Administering ArcGIS for Server

Installing and configuring ArcGIS for Server to publish, optimize, and secure GIS services

Hussein Nasser

BIRMINGHAM - MUMBAI

Administering ArcGIS for Server

First published: January 2014

Production Reference: 1170114

Published by Packt Publishing Ltd.
Livery Place
35 Livery Street
Birmingham B3 2PB, UK.

ISBN 978-1-78217-736-4

www.packtpub.com

Cover Image by Ravaji Babu (ravaji_babu@outlook.com)

Credits

Author

Hussein Nasser

Reviewers

Paul Crickard

Chandler Sterling

Tram Vu Khanh Truong

John (Yiguang) Zhang

Acquisition Editors

Rebecca Youe

Edward Gordon

Ashwin Nair

Lead Technical Editor

Anila Vincent

Technical Editors

Pratik More

Mrunmayee Patil

Rohit Kumar Singh

Copy Editors

Alisha Aranha

Brandt D'Mello

Gladson Monteiro

Adithi Shetty

Project Coordinator

Joel Goveya

Proofreaders

Faye Coulman

Lucy Rowland

Indexer

Tejal Soni

Graphics

Ronak Dhruv

Production Coordinator

Shantanu Zagade

Cover Work

Shantanu Zagade

Foreword

GIS is a mature industry, with its roots in the late 60s in forestry and county polygon maintenance through vector topology (others such as GRASS and IDRISI concentrated on the raster domain). Storing location and attribute information has been a challenge, not only since the early days of severely limited computing power and storage space, but even today in the management of ever-growing spatial and tabular repositories. This has been handled in several ways: two tenors being Esri Arc/Info separating the spatial and the tabular repositories, and Oracle Spatial embedding them in database tables. Esri evolved from the desktop to the server by offering SDE, a layer between its data and RDBMS that effectively spatialises database tables.

After the arrival of the Internet, further web services have been devised by commercial and open source technologies alike, but that is a subject in its own right? And while RDBMS scales hardware such as Oracle Exadata, as data expands to petabytes in real time, a whole other arena such as Amazon services or SAP in-memory addresses Big Data. But what about big geo data?

ArcGIS for Server is the third generation that adds a host of management, integrity, and performance tools designed to help implement scalable enterprise GIS.

Hussein is a geo enthusiast, whose chief concern is to make the "Gen 3" mid-section above amenable to geo experts and project engineers alike. As a practitioner in the field, he brings a deft touch to the ins-and-outs of this powerful yet complex offering. Esri being the de facto server geo standard, this book will benefit a wide array of infrastructure administrators and application engineers. Yet Hussein's clear prose explains it well enough; his first principles will allow his audience to apply their lessons learned to other platforms, and therein lies the "sweet spot":

> ArcGIS for Server offers interoperability to many other server
> and service platforms.

This book will thus be a great learning guide to help you understand the interconnectivity of data and applications. The biggest takeaway may be that readers will discover the "Internet of things" as a real-world paradigm, rather than just concepts "in the clouds" or "in the cloud". As an IT and poet friend once said: "Ladies and gentlemen… start your servers… and let the geo begin!"

Andrew Zolnai
blog.zolnai.ca
Cambridge, UK

About the Author

Hussein Nasser is an Esri award-winning Senior GIS Solution Architect at Electricity & Water Authority, Bahrain. In 2007, he won the first place at the annual ArcGIS for Server Code Challenge, conducted at the Esri Developer Summit in Palm Springs, California, for using AJAX technology with ArcGIS for Server, which was not implemented back then. He spent eight years as a GIS Architect at leading Middle Eastern engineering company Khatib & Alami, implementing various Utilities GIS systems based on Esri technology across the Middle East. Hussein then moved to a more focused environment at Electricity & Water Authority, Bahrain, his homeland, where he could channel his expertise to develop a robust GIS Utilities solution and fully integrate it with the e-government project to help Bahrain move towards the smart grid. In addition, Hussein is fascinated with peak research topics, including papers he is currently working on: *The Human API: A Software Interface to Prevent Cancer*, *Global Economic Crisis and Natural Disasters Quantum Detector*, and *Stock Market and the Moon Phase*.

Writing this book was not easy, however, having the closest people's support definitely made it enjoyable. I would like to thank my wife, Nada, who was patient and supportive throughout this journey; I would stay up at some nights while she made me my favorite tea, sometimes when I didn't write for a while she would fire up my laptop, prepare my tea, pair my headset to `stereomood.com`, and ask me to resume writing. She even sometimes forced me to take long breaks when I wrote too much. I would like to thank my mother for encouraging me to be the best in what I do and for her faith in me, which lights up in her eyes when I see her. I would like to finally thank my wise friend, Andrew, for pointing me in the right direction when I seemed lost. To my family and friends who knew about this book and encouraged me to finish it, thank you.

About the Reviewers

Paul Crickard is a systems administrator in Albuquerque, New Mexico. He has a master's degree in Political Science and has presented papers at the United States Naval Academy's Foreign Affairs Conference and the American Journalism Historians Association Regional Conference in Salt Lake City. He has given demonstrations on the use of Revit, BIM, and GIS to the Public School Facility Authority in New Mexico and the Albuquerque BIM505 users' group. Above all, he is loved and adored by his beautiful wife and son, without whom all other accolades pale in brilliance.

Chandler Sterling is a GIS Analyst for the City of Pasadena's Department of Information Technology in California. He attended the University of Wisconsin-Madison where he earned a graduate capstone certificate in GIS and a bachelor's degree in Geography and Political Science. He also co-founded an online resource hub for geospatial learning, the GIS Collective, which can be found at www.giscollective.org. He enjoys playing music with his band, The Electric West, and currently lives in Los Angeles.

Tram Vu Khanh Truong received her master's degree in Regional and City Planning at the University of Oklahoma and has worked in the planning field for almost four years. Currently, she is a Transportation Planner at the Greensboro Urban Area Metropolitan Planning Organization. Her duties include GIS development, data analysis, and Transportation System Planning. Tram Truong has a passion in utilizing GIS in transportation planning to support decision making and linking multimodal transportation planning with mixed use of land development planning.

John (Yiguang) Zhang has been in the geospatial industry for over 20 years with a strong background in GIS, photogrammetry, and remote sensing. He has been working as a GIS developer and analyst for the past 15 years and has experienced various GIS projects from start to finish on the GIS application design, development and implementation, GIS analysis, and map production. He has also managed complex spatial databases and experienced a lot of spatial data conversion and integration processes. His creative thinking skills have helped him solve problems effectively through the course of his career in public and private sectors, such as city of Chilliwack and Inergraph. He is proficient with Esri ArcGIS family products including ArcGIS Desktop and ArcGIS Server and spatial database management systems such as Oracle Spatial, SQL Server, and Open Source PostgreSQL/PostGIS. He is also competitive in .NET and Web 2.0 technologies. He holds a master's degree in Digital Photogrammetry and an advanced diploma in GIS from British Columbia Institute of Technologies, Canada.

Firstly, I'd like to thank my wife, Winnie, for dedicating her time in taking care of the family, and for her patience with this wonderful book review and other projects. I would also like to thank my son Sylvester and daughter Sylvia for their bright ideas to the problems I had to solve.

www.PacktPub.com

Support files, eBooks, discount offers and more

You might want to visit www.PacktPub.com for support files and downloads related to your book.

Did you know that Packt offers eBook versions of every book published, with PDF and ePub files available? You can upgrade to the eBook version at www.PacktPub.com and as a print book customer, you are entitled to a discount on the eBook copy. Get in touch with us at service@packtpub.com for more details.

At www.PacktPub.com, you can also read a collection of free technical articles, sign up for a range of free newsletters and receive exclusive discounts and offers on Packt books and eBooks.

http://PacktLib.PacktPub.com

Do you need instant solutions to your IT questions? PacktLib is Packt's online digital book library. Here, you can access, read and search across Packt's entire library of books.

Why Subscribe?

- Fully searchable across every book published by Packt
- Copy and paste, print and bookmark content
- On demand and accessible via web browser

Free Access for Packt account holders

If you have an account with Packt at www.PacktPub.com, you can use this to access PacktLib today and view nine entirely free books. Simply use your login credentials for immediate access.

Instant Updates on New Packt Books

Get notified! Find out when new books are published by following @PacktEnterprise on Twitter, or the *Packt Enterprise* Facebook page.

Table of Contents

Preface

If you are at a library and you grabbed this book, chances are that you have heard about ArcGIS for Server in a meeting and you want to know what this product is and what it is capable of. You might have picked up this book because you were explicitly asked by your manager to investigate the capability of this bleeding-edge technology and report with tangible results. Or maybe you are a system administrator who is in the middle of implementing ArcGIS for Server as your backbone architecture. Whether you are a curious blogger, a business developer, or a technical system analyst, I can guarantee that this book won't disappoint you.

Administering ArcGIS for Server was designed for all levels. You might get a satisfying definition of the product and its components, with comprehensive and straightforward illustrations, by reading the first chapter of this book. If you want to just test ArcGIS for Server, you can get it up and running in testing track—a quick, simple, and efficient method for installation—and do the exercises in most of the chapters. If you are planning to set up ArcGIS for Server on your production environment, you can fully read all of the chapters and appendices and explore the advanced security preferences and performance tips to make your setup run optimally.

What this book covers

Chapter 1, Best Practices for Installing ArcGIS for Server, introduces the product and illustrates its architecture and components. It then takes you through three tracks for installing the product: the simple testing track, the advanced tech-savvy production track, and finally the last track, which will show you how to set up and configure ArcGIS for Server specifically as a virtualized environment.

Chapter 2, Authoring Web Services, teaches you the concept behind a web service and different communication protocols. You will also learn how to author and publish GIS services so various clients can consume them.

Chapter 3, Consuming GIS Services, illustrates how to consume services that you learned to author and publish in the previous chapter. You will learn how to visualize, edit, and analyze services using different clients.

Chapter 4, Planning and Designing GIS Services, is where you will analyze requirements and plan what services you want to have. You then will use the planning result to design the services you nominated with rich UML tools. You will also learn to design the underlying geodatabase, which is the source that feeds these services.

Chapter 5, Optimizing GIS Services, shows you how to select the correct parameters and preferences that will make your ArcGIS for Server run at its optimal state. Optimization techniques such as pooling, process isolation, and caching can be applied to bring the most out of your ArcGIS for Server and make your services run much more efficiently and effectively.

Chapter 6, Clustering and Load Balancing, introduces the concept of clustering, a new technique that allows you to group machines into a cluster. You can then assign services to run on each cluster based on machine power, memory, or even on networking factors.

Chapter 7, Securing ArcGIS for Server, introduces different security mechanisms available on ArcGIS for Server. GIS-tier authentication, Web authentication, and HTTPS can be applied interchangeably, depending on the security level desired by your organization.

Chapter 8, Server Logs, will teach you how to harvest the logs and reports generated by ArcGIS for Server and use them to monitor your system effectively. There are different levels of logs, ranging from abstract to detailed, and the level you configure for your setup will depend on how thoroughly you want to monitor your ArcGIS for Server. Fine and detailed logs come with a performance penalty.

Appendix A, Selecting the Right Hardware, describes how to select the right hardware for your ArcGIS for Server environment by providing general rules of thumb. I have come up with formulas that you can use to calculate the number of cores and amount of memory required to serve your users.

Appendix B, Server Architecture, will display the difference between the old and the new ArcGIS for Server architecture. You are going to learn how ArcGIS for Server has survived the 32-bit architecture locking trap and migrated to the more effective 64-bit architecture.

What you need for this book

You need the following software for this book:

- A Browser, preferably Google Chrome, which you can download from `http://www.google.com/chrome`.

- Esri ArcGIS for Server 10.2 or 10.1, preferably 10.2, which you can download a trial of from `http://www.esri.com/software/arcgis/trial` or order from your local Esri distributor.

- Esri ArcGIS for Desktop 10.2 or 10.1, preferably 10.2, which you can download a trial of from `http://www.esri.com/software/arcgis/trial` or order from your local Esri distributor.

- Microsoft SQL Server Express 2012, which you can download for free from `http://www.microsoft.com/en-us/download/details.aspx?id=29062`.

- Oracle VirtualBox, which you can download for free from `https://www.virtualbox.org/`.

Who this book is for

Whether you are a GIS user, analyst, DBA, system administrator, or programmer with a basic knowledge of Esri GIS, this book is for you. Although the book is tailored to fit system administration and analyst requirements, users can find it equally useful. Each chapter segregates the advanced technical tips from the basic and required tasks. This makes it easier for users to perform only the necessary steps to run the software.

Conventions

In this book, you will find a number of styles of text that distinguish between different kinds of information. Here are some examples of these styles and an explanation of their meaning.

Code words in text are shown as follows: "Naturally, each GIS server generates its own logs and this is all saved by default at `C:\arcgisserver\logs\`."

A block of code is set as follows:

```
FINE Nov 17, 2013, 11:29:17 AM REST request received. Request size
is 178 characters. Parcels.MapServer
```

When we wish to draw your attention to a particular part of a code block, the relevant lines or items are set in bold:

```
<%
Dim r
Randomize (Timer)
r = Rnd()
r = r * 100
r = Round(r)
Response.Write(r)
%>
```

New terms and **important words** are shown in bold. Words that you see on the screen, in menus or dialog boxes for example, appear in the text like this: "From the **View Log Messages** panel, click on **Query** to view the current logfiles."

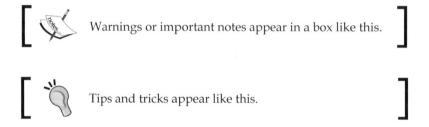

Warnings or important notes appear in a box like this.

Tips and tricks appear like this.

Reader feedback

Feedback from our readers is always welcome. Let us know what you think about this book—what you liked or may have disliked. Reader feedback is important for us to develop titles that you really get the most out of.

To send us general feedback, simply send an e-mail to feedback@packtpub.com and mention the book title via the subject of your message.

If there is a topic that you have expertise in and you are interested in either writing or contributing to a book, see our author guide at www.packtpub.com/authors.

Customer support

Now that you are the proud owner of a Packt book, we have a number of things to help you to get the most from your purchase.

Downloading the example code

You can download the example code files for all Packt books you have purchased from through account at `http://www.packtpub.com`. If you purchased this book elsewhere, you can visit `http://www.packtpub.com/support` and register to have the files e-mailed directly to you.

Errata

Although we have taken every care to ensure the accuracy of our content, mistakes do happen. If you find a mistake in one of our books—maybe a mistake in the text or the code—we would be grateful if you would report this to us. By doing so, you can save other readers from frustration and help us improve subsequent versions of this book. If you find any errata, please report them by visiting `http://www.packtpub.com/submit-errata`, selecting your book, clicking on the **errata submission form** link, and entering the details of your errata. Once your errata are verified, your submission will be accepted and the errata will be uploaded on our website, or added to any list of existing errata, under the *Errata* section of that title. Any existing errata can be viewed by selecting your title at `http://www.packtpub.com/support`.

Piracy

Piracy of copyright material on the Internet is an ongoing problem across all media. At Packt, we take the protection of our copyright and licenses very seriously. If you come across any illegal copies of our works, in any form, on the Internet, please provide us with the location address or website name immediately so that we can pursue a remedy.

Please contact us at `copyright@packtpub.com` with a link to the suspected pirated material.

We appreciate your help in protecting our authors' and our ability to bring you valuable content.

Questions

You can contact us at `questions@packtpub.com` if you are having a problem with any aspect of the book, and we will do our best to address it.

1
Best Practices for Installing ArcGIS for Server

ArcGIS for Server (hereafter known as **Server**) installation is a challenging task; use a parameter that does not fit your requirements, hardware, or operating system, and you will end up with a buggy launch, unexpected errors, and an unstable setup. This will eventually force you to waste precious time and resources reinstalling and reconfiguring the product. If you are an ArcGIS user, you will know the pain of having that one small problem which can only be fixed by completely reinstalling the product. Therefore, having the right configuration will help you save a lot of time later and result in a much healthier setup.

In this chapter, we will define the Server site, which holds all configurations, including **web servers**, **GIS servers**, **logfiles**, and **data stores**. Then, we will thoroughly explain the different installation tracks that you can select for ArcGIS for Server.

Installation tracks

There are three different installation tracks that we will offer in this book. The **Testing Installation Track** offers the typical installation with minimum configuration for those of you who wanted to test the technology. The **Production Installation Track** has the comprehensive and best practices configurations. And finally, the **Virtualized Environment Installation Track** shows how to configure Server specifically as a virtualized environment.

Testing Installation Track

If you are a student who wants to explore the ArcGIS technology or an employee who wants to introduce this product to his/her firm, or just have an older version of Server that you wish to upgrade, this is a good starting track for you. You can also select this track if any of the following criteria holds true for you:

- You have a workstation running Windows 8 or 7 and you want to test this product

- Performance doesn't matter for you at this stage

- You are not behind a proxy server

- You do not want to add multiple servers to your Server site

- You are not concerned about **load balancing**, a process of balancing the incoming requests across a spectrum of machines to ensure fair load distribution on each one of them

- You do not want to publish your services publicly online; rather, you want to use it on your local area network

- You have a very small user base, for whom you will probably write an HTML5 site to consume the services from your tablet or phone over Wi-Fi

Production Installation Track

If you already know the product capabilities or have performed a Testing Installation Track and you are ready to take your Server installation to the next level, go for Production Installation Track. If you have a powerful server linked to an **Active Directory Domain Controller**, which contains the users and roles for Windows, performance is a key element. You might add other GIS servers to your Server site later as your user base increases. This track will then help you harness the full power of Server.

Virtualized Environment Installation Track

For those who have never worked with virtualization before, virtualization is the process of breaking down a physical machine into multiple virtual machines that share the host's resources. You can choose to work with Virtualization Track if one of the following statements holds true for you:

- You do not have access to powerful physical machines, but your company provides you with powerful blade servers with a virtualization setup

- You are planning to add a couple or more virtual machines to your Server site along with some physical ones to boost your site

- You want to create multiple Server sites for testing purposes

- You want to install different versions of Server to check the compatibility with your database and ultimately select the correct version to install on your production environment

- You want to set up a preproduction environment where you want to simulate the production environment on virtual machines using the Production Installation Track

Although this option is good for testing, it is not recommended for a production environment. This chapter will discuss these three installation tracks in detail and will help you select the track that fits your needs for a successful installation of ArcGIS for Server.

The anatomy of the Server site

When you finish installing Server, which you will be doing in the coming pages, you will have a placeholder for your services; this placeholder is called the **site** (hereafter known as **Server site**). It is where all the configurations are saved. A Server site has its own configurations, services, GIS servers, web servers, and even security parameters that can be managed independently. It is where services will be published and where applications will connect to consume those services.

Server site components

A Server site consists of two main components: the Web server, which accepts the requests, and the GIS server, which processes them.

Web server

A Web server hosts many websites. Each website listens on a unique port on the Web server address using the HTTP protocol. For instance, if your Web server IP address is 10.0.0.6, the default website will initially listen on port 80, which is the default HTTP port. Consequently, you can access the website from a browser address bar by typing http://10.0.0.6:80, and since 80 is the default port for HTTP, you can safely remove it from the URL and it will appear as http://10.0.0.6.

HTTP

The Hypertext Transfer Protocol is a web protocol that deals with standards for rendering web pages on a web browser.

Port

A port is a virtual access entrance on a networked host machine that has a unique number on which connections can be established in order to exchange information between the host and remote machine.

Therefore, as long as the Web server 10.0.0.6 is accessible from a given network, you can access the website with any browser from any machine on that network. This is the main power of the Web server: install it in one place and access it from multiple locations using one address. We will explain how to set up a Web server in the Production Track.

A Web server is an essential part of an ArcGIS for Server installation. It receives client requests, translates them, forwards them to the GIS servers for processing, and then returns the results to the client. In a Web server, you can manage what clients should and should not access using customized security parameters, thus having more control over your content. In this book, we will be working with the Windows Web server **Internet Information Services (IIS)**.

IIS

Internet Information Services is a software that, when installed, turns the machine into a Web server that can listen to requests on ports and return appropriate responses, usually on port 80.

Starting with ArcGIS 10.1, Esri installs a hidden Web server along with each GIS server and creates a website listening on port 6080. We will discuss how to link this hidden Web server to a dedicated Web server on a different port in the Production Track.

GIS server

The GIS server does all the background work to serve a request. It handles tasks such as spatial operations, querying data, analysis, calculating results, and executing geoprocessing tasks such as buffering geometries. The GIS server then returns the processed result to the Web server, which feeds the information to the client who requested it. The GIS server will connect to the **Geodatabase**. If you are using an Enterprise geodatabase, you have to make sure you have the client **Database Management System (DBMS)** installed and configured correctly in each GIS server.

The GIS server executes the request while the Web server controls the traffic.

The GIS server is also where all the services are running; thus, it will be the one which requires the most resources.

DBMS

A DBMS is a system designed to store, retrieve, and process data from a distributed environment.

Geodatabase

Geographical Database is a relational database that is enabled by Esri to store and retrieve geographic fields and records and conduct geo-related tasks on them.

Server site management

A Server site can be managed by the primary administration account, which you will specify in the installation stage. Using the ArcGIS for Server Manager, which is a website that is installed with the Server and allows you to configure the Server site, you will be able to manage the following items in the Server site:

- Services
- Machines
- Output directories
- Configuration stores
- Clusters
- Data stores
- Extensions
- Logfiles

The preceding components are covered in the following sections.

Services

A service is a functionality that exposes certain data to be consumed by remote connections by a request. The **Services** tab in ArcGIS for Server Manager allows you to manage existing services and add new ones, control what resources should be allocated to what services, monitor service affinity, and recycle those services which drain your resources. We have a dedicated chapter on how to author and publish map services.

Machines

The **Machines** option will allow you to manage GIS servers, add more GIS servers to a Server site, take down some servers for maintenance, and take the load off servers with low resources. The GIS servers are the backbone of your Server site; you need to monitor them regularly.

Output directories

The output of your GIS server operations goes to output directories. It is important to make sure all your GIS servers have read/write access to these directories. You will learn how to do this later in the *Master GIS server installation* section under the *Software installation* section.

Configuration stores

Your GIS servers work according to a blueprint that you have provided them with. Similar to the output directories, this set of instructions should be accessible at all times by your GIS servers.

Clusters

Clustering in ArcGIS for Server is the process of grouping different machines together so that they can be treated as one unit. You can group your GIS servers into clusters to better manage your services. For instance, you may create a cluster and add your GIS servers with high resources (processor and memory) and name it Power cluster. Then create another cluster and add machines with lower specs and resources to it. You can then assign a high-affinity geoprocessing service to this Power cluster and your resourceful GIS servers will execute requests made to that service. This way, the other services can work comfortably on the default cluster. We will discuss more about clusters in *Chapter 6, Clustering and Load Balancing*.

Clustering is the opposite of virtualization. Clustering merges different machines together to act as one, while virtualization breaks down a single machine into a group of machines.

Data stores

GIS servers will occasionally require establishing connections to geodatabases. It is recommended that you register these databases in the data store, which we will be doing in *Chapter 2*, *Authoring Web Services*, so that your servers can connect to it. Otherwise, the data will have to be copied locally on each GIS server, which might introduce inconsistencies and performance penalties.

Extensions

Just like ArcGIS for Desktop, ArcGIS for Server allows developers to customize server functionality and extend its capabilities. This option will allow you to register an extension to Server.

Logfiles

The **Logfiles** tab allows you to see how your GIS servers are doing, analyze the output logfiles on each server, and see what errors emerge so that you can fix them. You may measure the performance of a server by checking the response time between a request and the result. *Chapter 8*, *Server Logs*, is a dedicated chapter to learn all there is to know about logfiles.

Testing Installation Track

The advantage of Testing Installation Track is that it is compact and efficient. If you don't know where to start, this is probably a good starting point. ArcGIS for Server can run on any machine as long as the hardware and operating system are supported. That is why this track does not necessarily require a powerful machine; your Windows workstation or laptop will suffice. We will discuss the minimum ArcGIS for Server requirements in the next topic.

This section will guide you through the installation of Server on your PC or laptop with minimum configuration. Your machine will play two roles — the Web server and the GIS server — so it will receive client requests, process them, and return the result. If you are looking to break down the two roles across multiple servers, you should look at the *Production Installation Track* section, where you will be introduced to advanced installation configurations.

This track will get you up and running to test the product, publish services, and develop applications. The Testing Installation Track is sufficient to complete almost all the exercises in this book.

Server requirements

Any software tends to have certain minimum system requirements to function properly. This is due to Moor's law, which states that computing power doubles every 18 months, and as this power increases, software demands more system resources.

System requirements

ArcGIS for Server supports various operating systems; some are recommended for production environments, while others can be used for testing and are classified as follows.

Recommended for production

- Windows Server 2012 Standard and Datacenter (64-bit EM64T)
- Windows Server 2008 R2 Standard, Enterprise, and Datacenter (64-bit EM64T) SP1
- Windows Server 2008 Standard, Enterprise, and Datacenter (64-bit EM64T) SP2
- Windows Server 2003 Standard, Enterprise, and Datacenter (64-bit EM64T) SP2
- Red Hat Enterprise Linux Server 6
- Red Hat Enterprise Linux Server 5, update 7 + libX11 patch
- SUSE Linux Enterprise Server 11 SP1

Recommended for education, testing, and demo

- Windows 8 Basic, Professional, and Enterprise (64-bit EM64T)
- Windows 7 Ultimate, Enterprise, Professional, and Home Premium (64-bit EM64T) SP2
- Windows Vista Ultimate, Enterprise, Business, and Home Premium (64-bit EM64T) SP2
- Windows XP Professional Edition and Home Edition (64-bit EM64T) SP2

Best practice

Using Windows 7 or 8 to run Server in your production environment is not recommended because they are not designed to support high network access as Windows Server.

Although ArcGIS for Desktop is not mandatory for the installation of Server, you will need it when authoring and publishing services.

Hardware requirements

ArcGIS for Server requires a 64-bit instruction-set CPU in order to run. You can get Server to run comfortably on a dual-core, 64-bit processor with a 2 GB RAM machine running Windows XP 64-bit.

Software installation

For this installation, I used an Intel Core i7-2600 CPU Quad Core processor at 3.40 GHz and a 6 GB RAM PC running Windows 7 Professional 64-bit Service Pack 1. Make sure you have your ArcGIS for Server media disc ready and your license file in place. You can request a trial media disc from your local Esri distributer or download a trial from this link: http://www.esri.com/software/arcgis/trial. In this book, we will be installing ArcGIS for Server Version 10.2. Uninstall any ArcGIS products prior to 10.2; otherwise, you will run into complications.

Some components in ArcGIS for Server require Microsoft .NET framework. It is recommended that you install Version 3.5 or higher before you start.

First, log in to your machine using a Windows account with administrative privileges. Run the ESRI.exe file in your media installation disc and select the **ArcGIS for Server** option. If this is a fresh installation, you will be prompted to install one component (**GIS Server**). As explained earlier, installing this will turn your machine into a GIS server, and this GIS server will be bundled with a built-in Web server. We will discuss how to install a Web server on a dedicated machine in the *Production Installation Track* section.

Also make sure that the subfeature **.NET Extension Support** is selected for installation, and then click on **Next** as shown in the following screenshot.

 If you do not have .NET framework installed, you will not see the **.NET Extension Support** subfeature.

.NET Extension Support is necessary if you are planning to develop .NET applications on top of ArcGIS for Server.

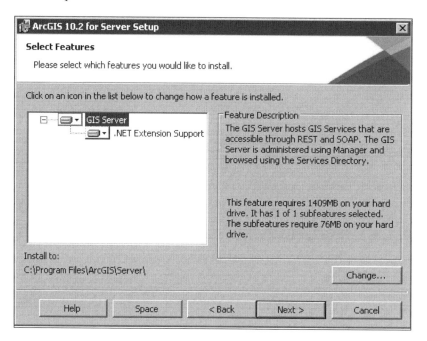

The hosted services on your server require a Windows account to run. This account doesn't have to be an administrator on the local machine; any account that is a member of user's group will suffice. We will later assign the proper privileges to this account in order to access the resources on the GIS server. You may use an existing local user on your machine or create a new one. To make things simple, you can let the installation create a new user.

In the **ArcGIS Server Account** field, type gisServer. In the **Password** and **Confirm Password** fields, enter a new password for a new account, and then click on **Next** as shown in the following screenshot:

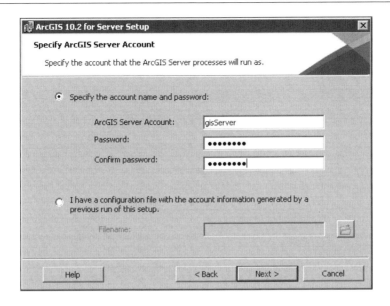

You can optionally export this configuration, which includes the ArcGIS for Server Windows account information in case you will be installing multiple GIS servers or planning to reinstall your product in the future. Select **Export configuration file** and select where you want to save it. Name it `local.gisServer.xml` so that you know that the account name is `gisServer` and it is on your local machine rather than a Windows domain.

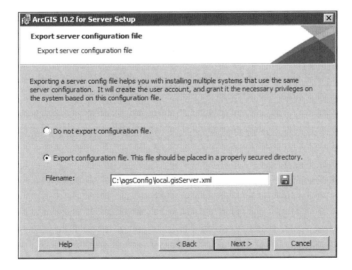

Now that all files are copied, authorization is required to fully complete your GIS server setup. Follow the steps to authorize the product if you have the license file (it is usually a copy protection file with the extension `.ecp`).

 You can access the authorization wizard from the Start menu if you choose to cancel it in during the installation.

You are now ready to start configuring ArcGIS for Server. The installation has created a new Windows account named `gisServer` on the machine as shown in the following screenshot:

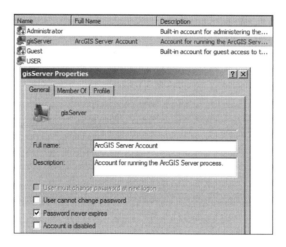

If you take a look at Task Manager, a Windows tool that allows you to monitor the performance of your machine, you will see that this account is running five processes. These processes will increase as you start publishing services. You can access Task Manager by pressing the *Ctrl* + *Alt* + *Del* keys.

ArcGISServer.exe	gisServer	00	61,128 K	44	ArcGISServer EXE
rmid.exe	gisServer	00	16,844 K	24	Java(TM) Platform SE binary
conhost.exe	gisServer	00	1,408 K	1	Console Window Host
cmd.exe	gisServer	00	1,376 K	1	Windows Command Processor
javaw.exe	gisServer	00	171,040 K	40	Java(TM) Platform SE binary

Configuring Server site

Now that the software is up and running, we will create our Server site to hold the configurations. Remember when we said that there is a built-in Web server with this installation? You are about to connect to it.

Working with ArcGIS for Server is more convenient using the Google Chrome browser. Chrome loads the sites on the local area network much faster and uses less memory. You can download Google Chrome at `http://www.google.com/chrome`.

Start Chrome, type `http://localhost:6080/arcgis/manager` in the address bar, and press *Enter*.

You may use your machine IP instead of `localhost` as follows:

`http://192.168.1.6:6080/arcgis/manager`

You can find out your IP by running `IPConfig` in the command prompt.

This is your Server site Manager; it is a website installed by the software and hosted on the built-in Web server running on port `6080`. It is recommended that you bookmark this page because you will be visiting it frequently. If this is the first time you visit this page after a fresh installation, you will be prompted with the following message:

This machine does not currently participate in an ArcGIS Server site. You can either create a new site or join an existing site.

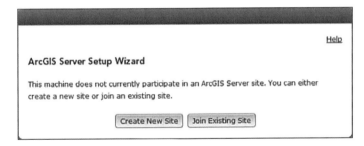

Since we do not have an existing Server site, we will go ahead and create a new one. Click on **Create New Site**.

This is an option that you can't undo. If you created a new site and you want to delete or change it to point to an existing one, you have to completely uninstall the software or use the admin API, which will be introduced in *Chapter 7, Securing ArcGIS for Server*.

A Server site requires an administrator to manage the site configuration. The **Primary Site Administrator** is created by the Server site configuration for you to use. Whenever you open ArcGIS for Server Manager, you have to enter these credentials to log in. This is not a Windows account like the one we configured before.

 The Primary Site Administrator is an account managed internally by the Server site; it is not related to the operating system.

Type the name of the administrator account in the **Username** field; you may use any name, but I recommend using `siteadmin`. Then type in a new password in the **Password** and the **Confirm Password** fields, and then click on **Next** as shown in the following screenshot:

Next, we will set up the directories of the site that the GIS server will be using. We will use the default settings here since we are using Testing Installation Track. In the **Root Server Directory** field, make sure the path is `C:\arcgisserver\directories`, and in the **Configuration Store** field, that the path is `C:\arcgisserver\config-store`. Click on **Next** as shown in the following screenshot:

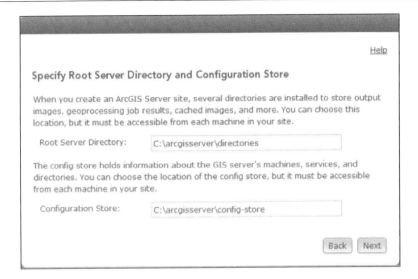

These directories will constantly be accessed by the GIS server Windows account, in our case, **gisServer**. That is why this user should have read/write access to the folder `C:\arcgisserver\` and all its subfolders.

You are ready to create the Server site. A summary of your configuration will be displayed; click on **Finish**. When this is complete, you have successfully installed ArcGIS for Server.

Production Installation Track

Your organization might want a high availability robust setup that can serve many users. This means you might need more than one GIS server on your Server site. You may want a dedicated Web server that you can configure so that you can publish your services on the public World Wide Web more securely. This requires applying security measures, **network load balancing (NLB)**, or **failover clusters**. The Production Installation Track equips you with necessary knowledge, tools, and best practices to ensure a stable production setup. You can also use this track for your preproduction testing environment, where you can simulate your setup in a virtualized environment and then replicate the installation on the actual production environment. If you are planning to use virtual machines, you can read through the *Virtualized Environment Installation Track* section to learn how to set up a virtual machine for Server.

Active Directory Domain Controller (ADDC)

ADDC is required to perform this installation.

NLB

NLB is the ability to balance network traffic between two or more nodes by using a virtual address.

Failover cluster

Also known as a high available cluster, a failover cluster is a group of servers arranged together to provide minimum downtime. If a server is down, another server from the cluster takes over.

Server requirements

Unlike Testing Installation Track, you need at least three servers for the Production Installation Track. The following is the configuration I will be using in this track:

Machine Name	Operating System	Description
WEB SERVER01	Windows Server 2008 R2 SP1 x64	Web Server and Configuration Store
GIS-SERVER01	Windows Server 2008 R2 SP1 x64	First GIS server
GIS-SERVER02	Windows Server 2008 R2 SP1 x64	Second GIS server

You may create virtual machines to mimic the three servers; refer to the *Virtualized Environment Installation Track* section to learn how to create the virtual machines.

System requirements

We will require one Web server and two GIS servers running any of the following operating systems:

- Windows Server 2012 Standard and Datacenter (64-bit EM64T)

- Windows Server 2008 R2 Standard, Enterprise, and Datacenter (64-bit EM64T) SP1

- Windows Server 2008 Standard, Enterprise, and Datacenter (64-bit EM64T) SP2

- Windows Server 2003 Standard, Enterprise, and Datacenter (64-bit EM64T) SP2

Esri no longer supports Windows Server 2003. Even if you manage to get it to work, I strongly recommend upgrading to Windows 2008 or later.

Hardware requirements

ArcGIS for Server requires a 64-bit instruction-set CPU in order to run. Your Server can run effectively on a quad-core 64-bit processor with minimum 8 GB of RAM. Although, as services and users increase, the 8 GB will be drained quickly. A 16 GB RAM GIS server can serve up to 100 users if you were planning to have five services on one GIS server. You can replace that GIS server with two 8 GB RAM as well. I have developed a rule of thumb to determine how much memory you require for each GIS server.

$$R = \frac{S.U}{20G\sqrt{3}}$$

Here, the variables represent the following values:

Variable	Description
R	RAM in Gigabytes
S	Maximum number of services anticipated
U	Maximum number of users expected (non-concurrent)
G	Number of GIS servers on the site

As we can see from the previous table, R is the minimum amount of memory in a single GIS server to make an optimal setup, S is the number of web services you are planning to have, U is the maximum number of users you expect, and G is the number of GIS servers that will split the load. If you would like to learn more, you can read through *Appendix A*, *Selecting the Right Hardware*, where I explain this formula thoroughly; there are also some tips on which hardware is best for your production environment.

Software installation

To install Server, we will first start with configuring Active Directory. Then we will install the first GIS server and then configure the Server site. After that, we will install the second GIS server and join the existing Server site, and we will finish by installing and configuring the dedicated web-server using the **Web Adaptor**.

Web Adaptor
A Web Adaptor is a bridge that integrates your dedicated Web server with the built-in Web server of ArcGIS for Server. It allows packets to be forwarded between the two web servers.

Active Directory configuration

Active Directory controls the security and policies of all Windows users, and it is very effective for ArcGIS for Server. Using Active Directory, create YOURDOMAIN\ arcgis.server on your domain—I will be using the GIS domain. To add the user to active directory, open **Active Directory Users and Computers** by navigating to **Start | Control Panel | Administrative Tools | Active Directory Users and Computers**. After that, perform the following steps:

1. In the console tree, right-click on the folder to which you want to add a user account.

2. Navigate to **Active Directory Users and Computers | domain node | folder**.

3. Click on **New**, and then click on **User**.

4. In the **First name** field, type the user's first name.

5. In the **Initials** field, type the user's initials.

6. In the **Last name** field, type the user's last name.

7. Modify the **Full name** field to add initials or reverse order of first and last names.

8. In **User logon name**, type the user's logon name, click on the **UPN** suffix in the drop-down list, and then click on **Next**.

9. In the **Password** and **Confirm password** fields, type the user's password. You will use this password for GIS server installation later.

Now, we need to add GIS\arcgis.server to the administrators group on the three servers WEB SERVER01, GIS-SERVER01, and GIS-SERVER02.

1. Log in to the server with an administrator user.

2. From the Start menu, click on **Run** and type compmgmt.msc to run **Computer Management**.

3. Go to **Local Users and Groups**.

4. Click on **Groups**.

5. Double-click on **Administrators**.

6. Click on **Add** and then type in your domain user GIS\arcgis.server.

Perform these steps on all three of your servers.

 The administrator privilege exists just to perform the installation; you can safely revoke the administrator privilege from this user after the installation.

GIS server installation

There are two installation steps. Master server installation is where we will create our Server site. The secondary installation is to join the rest of the servers to this master installation site.

Master GIS server installation

Log in to the master GIS server `GIS-SERVER01` with the user ID `GIS\arcgis.server`; this is a very important step for your site to be added to Active Directory.

 If you used another local user profile to perform the installation, you will end up with an inconsistent setup.

Run the `ESRI.exe` file and select the **ArcGIS for Server** setup. If this is a new installation, you will be prompted to install one component (**GIS Server**) as explained in the *Testing Installation Track* section. Installing this component will turn your server into a GIS server. This server is bundled with a built-in Web server running on port `6080`; make sure that the subfeature **.NET Extension Support** is selected for installation and then click on **Next**.

The hosted services on your server require a Windows account so that they can run silently on your GIS server. We will use our domain user `GIS\arcgis.server`. In the **ArcGIS Server Account** field, type `GIS\arcgis.server`, and in the **Password** and **Confirm Password** fields, enter the user's password, then click on **Next**.

 You have already created the user `GIS\arcgis.server` in Active Directory. Therefore, you should specify the password you used while creating the user.

Since we are going to set up another GIS server in exactly the same way, we will export this configuration, which includes the ArcGIS for Server Windows account information. Select **Export configuration file** and choose where you want to save it. Give it a name that corresponds with `YOURDOMAIN.arcgis.server.xml`, just so you know that this configuration file is associated with the Windows domain user `arcgis.server`. I named mine `GIS.arcgis.server.xml`.

Now that all files are copied, authorization is required to fully complete your GIS server setup. Follow the steps to authorize the product if you have the license file. You are now ready to start configuring ArcGIS for Server.

This account is running five processes. These processes will increase as you start authoring services.

Configuring Server site

Now that the software is up and running, we will create our Server site to hold the configurations. Since we still haven't installed our Web server, we will temporarily connect to the built-in Web server to set up our Server site. Open Chrome and type this in this address: `http://GIS-SERVER01:6080/arcgis/manager`.

Best practice

Using the IP address increases network performance by slightly more than 10 percent because it saves your network the trouble of resolving the machine name to the IP address. However, for demonstration purposes in this book, I will be using the machine name instead.

This is ArcGIS for Server Manager, a website hosted on the built-in Web server running on port `6080` used to manage the Server site. It is recommended that you bookmark this page because you will be visiting it frequently. If this is the first time you visit this page after a fresh installation, you will be prompted with a message:

This machine does not currently participate in an ArcGIS Server site. You can either create a new site or join an existing site.

Since we do not have an existing Server site anywhere in our network, we will create a new one. Click on **Create New Site**.

Any Server site needs to have an administrator, the Primary Site Administrator, who has the privileges to manage the site configuration, and whose credentials must be entered to log in to the site. This is not a Windows account like the one we configured earlier. Type `siteadmin` as the name of the administrator account in the **Username** field. Then type a new password in the **Password** and the **Confirm password** fields, and then click on **Next**. This will create the Primary Site Administrator with the specified credentials.

The directories and the configuration store of the site are a crucial part in the ArcGIS for Server setup. As explained earlier, those directories are accessed by the GIS servers, so they have to be available at all times. The best way to ensure that is to have **Network Attached Storage (NAS)** set up on your network and create all your directories on. If you don't have a NAS server, you can use any other server for storage. In this case, we will use the Web server as it is a highly available server and it is less likely to go down, unlike the GIS servers.

NAS

NAS is a data storage computer that provides file-level access to a network by a group of nodes.

One of the problems I faced with a client was that the load balancing between GIS servers was not working. The reason was that they were using one of the GIS servers as the configuration store. When they took that particular server out of the network for maintenance, the other GIS servers didn't take over because the configuration store and all the directories are no longer accessible by the other GIS servers.

Best practice

Do not use any of your GIS servers as a configuration store since they are highly likely to go down, thus bringing all of your architecture down as well. You will also not be able to take down that server from your site for maintenance.

In this exercise, we will use the Web server as our configuration store. Log in to your Web server `WEB SERVER01` using the `GIS\arcgis.server` Windows account. Go to the C drive and create a folder named `arcgisserver`. Share this folder and give it read/write to the `GIS\arcgis.server` domain user.

Go back to the installation, In the **Root Server Directory** field, type the path `\\WEB SERVER01\arcgisserver\directories`, and in the **Configuration Store** field, type `\\WEB SERVER01\arcgisserver\config-store`. Click on **Next**.

Since the user `GIS\arcgis.server` has read/write access to the folder `\\WEB SERVER01\arcgisserver\directories`, the GIS server will be able to access it as well.

Now, you are ready to create the master Server site. A summary of your configuration will be displayed; click on **Finish**. This takes a few minutes to get done.

Secondary GIS server installation

Now that the master Server site is created, it is ready to be joined by other GIS servers. It is important to understand that the master site is not located on GIS-SERVER01; rather, it is located in the configuration store which in turn is located in the arcgiserver directory on the WEB SERVER01 machine.

 The Server site is mistaken to be located on the master GIS server; in fact, it is saved in the configuration store.

Log in to the secondary GIS-SERVER02 machine using the GIS\arcgis.server Windows account and follow the same steps you performed in the master installation. Install GIS server and make sure **.NET Extension** is selected. This will install the GIS server component along with the Web server running on port 6080.

When you reach the **Specify ArcGIS for Server Account** form, copy the configuration file GIS.arcgis.server.xml we created previously into this machine, and select it so you don't need to re-enter the GIS\arcgis.server account. Continue the installation and authorize your server; click on **Next** to start configuring the site.

Configuring a secondary GIS server

Remember, we do not need to create another Server site since we have an existing one. All we need to do is to configure the built-in Web server of GIS-SERVER02 to point to our existing master site. Open Chrome, type http://GIS-SERVER02:6080/arcgis/manager in the address bar and press *Enter*.

This is your Server site Manager; you will be prompted with this message: **This machine does not currently participate in an ArcGIS Server site. You can either create a new site or join an existing site.** We do have an existing site, so click on **Join an Existing Site**.

In the **Specify Site URL** form, enter the master site address `http://GIS-SERVER01:6080` in the **ArcGIS Server Site URL** field; in the **Username** field, enter `siteadmin`, the primary administrator name, and in the **Password** field, enter the password for **siteadmin**; then click on **Next**.

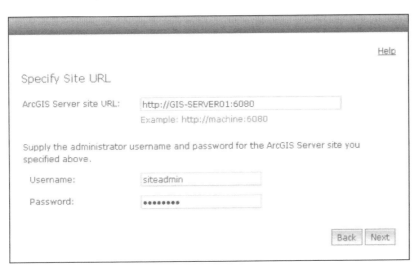

After you complete this successfully, you will have one site with two GIS servers ready to crunch services. You can manage this site by accessing any of the GIS server built-in web servers using any one of the following URLs:

- `http://GIS-SERVER01:6080/arcgis/manager`
- `http://GIS-SERVER02:6080/arcgis/manager`

What if you want to join a third machine? Which URL should you use, GIS-SERVER01 or GIS-SERVER02? The answer is that any will work, because both are joined to the same site.

 Once a GIS server joins a Server site, it inherits all the configurations of that site.

Web server installation

Now that you have finished your GIS server installation, you need to reinforce some access-management policies and control who can access what. To do that, the built-in web servers on your GIS servers are not enough; you need a dedicated Web server. It is not recommended that you install the Web server on the same machine as the GIS servers. GIS servers have high affinity, they consume a large portion of memory and CPU, and they are highly likely to go down. GIS servers are subject to regular maintenance, which means they have to be restarted from time to time, especially to install software updates or patches. If the machine hosting both the GIS server and Web server goes down for any of those reasons, your entire architecture will collapse. The rest of the GIS servers will be rendered useless since your users can no longer access the Web server that directs the traffic. While it is on a dedicated server, in-case one GIS server fails, it will re-route user traffic to the next available GIS server.

Best practice

Never install your Web server on a machine running as a GIS server, always use a dedicated machine as your Web server.

Even on a dedicated machine, a Web server might still go down. To prevent this, you may install an NLB node with two web servers instead of one.

Configuring the end user Web Adaptor

You have your own Web server software (IIS), and ArcGIS for Server has its own 6080 Web server; we need a way to make these two understand and forward information to each other. For that, we will install a Web Adaptor. You can install as many Web Adaptors as you want, thus creating different websites to be managed independently.

You can now log in to WEB SERVER01 using the GIS\arcgis.server Windows account. From your ArcGIS for Server media disk, run ESRI.EXE and select **ArcGIS Web Adaptor (IIS)**. If you do not have IIS installed on your machine, the software will do it for you. This is valid when you have ArcGIS for Server 10.1 SP1 or higher; otherwise, you have to install IIS manually. In the **Select Features** options, make sure **Cross-Domain Policy Files** is unchecked.

Cross domain

Cross-domain policy is the behavior by which a web application running on machine "A" requests information from another machine "B". This can introduce various security vulnerabilities. Esri doesn't mention this, but enabling cross-domain policy files opens a security flaw on your server; if you do not have a good reason to enable it, keep it disabled.

Esri recommends enabling cross-domain policy because Silverlight and Flex viewers need it in order to function. Since we will use neither in our exercises, you will not need this option as shown in the following screenshot:

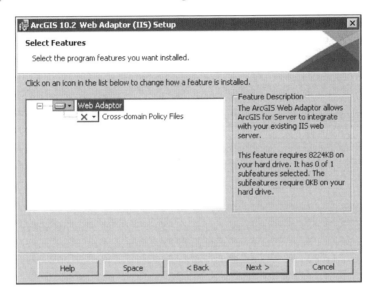

Click on **Next** to view the next form, where you will configure the virtual directory for your Web Adaptor.

Best practice

Enabling **Cross Domain Policy Files** on the Web server allows attackers to inject harmful code using **Cross Side Scripting (XSS)** on websites hosted on the Web server, which might allow them to send and receive sensitive information from a remote server.

The Web Adapter will create a new virtual directory on your Web server, and all your services will go under this directory. In the **New Virtual Directory** form, type wa—short for Web Adaptor—in the **Name of the ArcGIS Web Adaptor** field, and then click on **Next**.

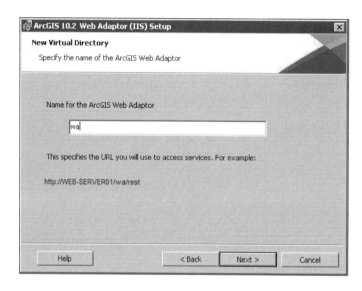

Now that the Web Adaptor is installed, we need to join it to the Server site. Launch Chrome and type this address in the address bar: http://WEB SERVER01:6080/wa/webadaptor.

Starting with 10.2, the Web Adaptor is used to configure **Portal for ArcGIS**, another product Esri is currently focusing on along with ArcGIS for Server. This is why you will be prompted to select which product you want to configure; select **ArcGIS for Server** and click on **Next**. You will be prompted to join the web adaptor to the Server site. Here, we need to specify a URL that will point to our master Server site. In our case, both http://GIS-SERVER01:6080 and http://GIS-SERVER02:6080 point to the same site; therefore, using any of them will work. In the **GIS Server URL** field, type http://GIS-SERVER01:6080; in the **Administrator Username** field, type siteadmin, which is the site primary administrator; and in the **Administrator Password** field, type the password. Click on **Configure**.

Make sure the **Enable administrative access to your site through the Web Adaptor** checkbox is unchecked. It is recommended that you disable end users to have access to the site manager and change site configurations. We will separately create another adaptor especially for administrators.

Once you click on **Configure**, and you will get the following message:

The following GIS Servers are registered to your Web Adaptor

GIS-SERVER01

GIS-SERVER02

Your end users can now access the GIS servers through the Web server with the URL `http://WEB SERVER01/wa/rest/services`. They do not need to worry about port `6080`, and they need not know your GIS servers. Note that when you try to access the manager with the URL `http://WEB SERVER01/wa/manager`, you will get this error message:

Administrator access is disabled.

Please contact your system administrator to enable it.

Best practice

Do not enable administrator access through the Web Adaptor that the end users will be using.

Configuring the administrator Web Adaptor

You can optionally configure a dedicated web adaptor with administrative access.

Follow the same steps as in the *Configuring the end user Web Adaptor* section and give the adaptor the name waadmin. In the last step, just enable the administrator for this site. Try to access the manager via http://WEB SERVER01/waadmin/manager.

You just completed a full-fledged robust installation of ArcGIS for Server.

Virtualized Environment Installation Track

You may want to try ArcGIS for Server but may not have a free machine or may have a Mac OS X machine, which the product does not support yet. Perhaps you do not want to install Server on a production environment until you simulate the entire setup. If either of this is the case, you can use the virtualization track installation. This track will walk you through setting up and cloning virtual machines. We will be using the open source Oracle Virtual Box to set up three Windows Server 2008 R2 virtual machines. Then, you can follow the same installation tips we discussed in the *Production Installation Track* section.

You can also use VMWare vSphere 4 and 5 as they are supported.

Installing Oracle Virtual Box

Go to `http://www.virtualbox.org` and download the version that matches your operating system. Since I'm using Mac OS, I downloaded Virtual Box for Mac. After the download, install the software using the typical settings.

Adding a new virtual machine

To add a new virtual machine, you need to specify certain configurations, such as the memory and hard drive size. Open Oracle Virtual Box and click on the **New** button. Click on the **Hide Description** button. In the **Name** field, type `GIS-SERVER01`; this is the virtual machine name and not the computer name, so you have to go later and change the computer name as well. In the **Type** drop-down list, select **Microsoft Windows**, and in the **Version** drop-down list, select **Windows 2008 (64 bit)**. In the **Memory size** box, select the size of the virtual machine RAM. I will go with the default **512 MB**: that will be enough for a virtual machine, but you may increase it if you have enough memory. In the **Hard drive** box select **Create a virtual hard drive now** and then click on **Create**.

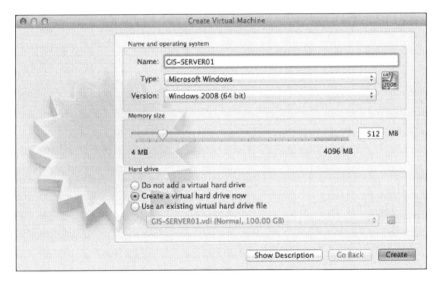

The **Create a virtual hard drive now** option is where you specify the hard drive information. In the file location box leave it to **GIS-SERVER01**. Type 80 GB in the **File size** box, which should be enough for a typical GIS server; select the **VDI (Virtual Box Disk Image)** type and set the storage to **Dynamically allocated**, which will allocate the physical hard drive size. Click on **Create** to create the drive.

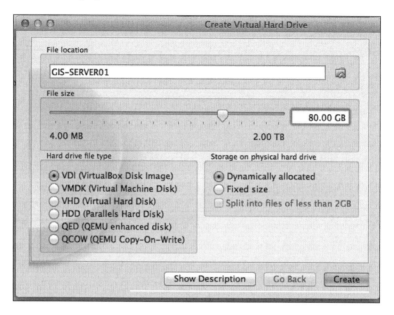

Now, we have an empty virtual machine with no operating system. What is left to install is the operating system. If you have a Windows 2008 R2 media disk you can insert it in the DVD drive and run the virtual machine installation normally. If you do not have a media disc and you have an ISO image instead, you can create a virtual CD on your virtual machine. From the **Oracle Virtual Box** settings, click on **Storage**, and then right-click on the **Controller IDE** option and select **Add CD/DVD Device**. Select **Choose from file** and select your ISO image. You can now continue installing Windows normally.

After the Windows installation is completed, make sure to change the computer name to GIS-SERVER01.

 You can change the machine name in **System Properties** under **Computer Name**.

Now that you have configured your virtual machine successfully, do not install any ArcGIS products yet; keep it as a raw Windows installation so that we can clone it into two machines. Now we will clone GIS-SERVER01 into two other machines (GIS-SERVER02 and WEB SERVER01).

Cloning a virtual machine

We did most of the work on one machine, where we configured the memory and hard disc size and Windows installation. Instead of repeating these steps, we can simply clone our existing machine into multiple identical machines.

To clone a virtual machine, it should be turned off. Shut down your virtual machine if it is running, and then right-click on the virtual machine icon and select **Clone**. In the **Clone Virtual Machine** window, perform the following steps:

1. Click on the **Hide Description** button.
2. Type the name of the new machine—GIS-SERVER02.
3. Check the **Reinitialize the MAC addresses of all network cards** checkbox.
4. Select **Full Clone** so that we can get an exact copy of GIS-SERVER01 with a new hard drive, and in the **Snapshots** box, select **Everything**.
5. Click on **Clone**.

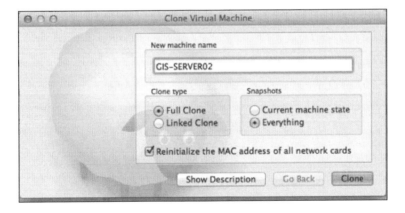

You can perform the same steps to create the WEB SERVER01 virtual machine. Now you can install ArcGIS for Server as done in the Production Installation Track setup procedures using the virtual machines.

Summary

In this chapter, you used some of the best practices for installing a robust setup for ArcGIS for Server. There were three tracks. The Testing Installation Track features a simple and typical installation with minimum configuration for testing the technology, The Production Installation Track has comprehensive explanations of all the options in Server—we covered the best practices for the configurations that should and shouldn't be used depending on your requirements. Finally, in the last track you learnt how to set up and configure Server specifically for virtualized environments.

In the next chapter, we will learn how to author and publish web services for ArcGIS for Server.

2

Authoring Web Services

Web services are the medium by which ArcGIS for Server communicates. They are the cogs that drive Server and feed your end users. ArcGIS for Server supports many types of web services. Each of these types implement an international standard, which is supported by various clients. Before we go through these standards or protocols, we will first define what a web service is. Then, you will create your first web service using the classic **Active Server Pages** (**ASP**). This exercise will cement the idea of web services and will let you further understand how they work. It will also prepare you for the second part of this chapter where you will learn how to author web services specifically for Server. The services that you will be publishing on Server are a little different from the classical web services. They have a geographic flavor to it. This is why throughout this chapter, we will refer to web services published on Server as **GIS services**.

The classical web service

In a nutshell, a web service is a method that can be called by a client to perform a particular task and return some results. Such results can be in plain text, as links, or media that can be interpreted by browsers. What makes it different from any regular method is that this method is a **cross platform**, which means you can call it from practically anywhere and get the output in a convenient and native format. For example, you spend countless hours to develop an algorithm on C# that performs a certain task. Your boss is happy, and she/he asks you to deploy it on your Unix database server. However, there is a slight problem here. C# code uses the Microsoft .NET Framework that happens to run only on the Microsoft Windows operating system; therefore, it is a challenging task to port this algorithm to Unix. One solution will be to rewrite the algorithm to run on Unix, which will lead to two versions of the code scattered on multiple locations. However, this will introduce more maintenance work, which is not very efficient. Another solution is to deploy this algorithm as a web service, since web services use HTTP. You will be able to call this algorithm not only from Unix but also from practically any other platform.

It is a de facto that a web service should follow a known standard or protocol so clients can easily communicate with it and consume it. For instance, HTTP follows certain code for communicating between a client and server. You can choose to adopt this protocol and therefore all the clients who use HTTP can consume your service. There are cases where you want to create your own protocol. For instance, your web service contains sensitive data and supporting HTTP might compromise it. So your new protocol, let's call it X encrypts communications, so only clients who support protocol X can read this web service. I usually explain web service protocols by comparing it with the languages we speak. For example, I have chosen to write this book in the English language in favor of Arabic because English is a universal language and thus more readers would acquire this book. I can also write another edition of this book in Arabic, thus supporting two languages and increase my reader base.

Creating a classical web service

There are a number of protocols developed for web services. Before you go through these protocols, it is a good practice to know how classical web services work without a protocol. To tackle that, you will be creating your own raw web service from scratch. This way you will truly be able to grasp the idea behind web services' standards and then comfortably work with one without wondering about its mechanics. We will need a machine that runs IIS to do the following task. The machine WEB-SERVER01 that we created in the previous chapter will do fine.

Random numbers are used in so many applications. They are used during encryptions and for generating a passcode. In this exercise, we will create a sample web service that will return a random number.

 ASP is a Microsoft server-side scripting language that is used to create dynamic content web pages.

Enabling ASP on IIS

In some cases, ASP might be turned off on the Web server, so we will make sure it is on. From the **Server Manager** window, select **Roles** and then **Web Server** (IIS). From the window on the right pane, scroll down and click on **Add Roles Services**. A new form will be displayed under the **Application Development** tree node; check the **ASP** box. Click on **Next** and then **Install** to install the required options for ASP.

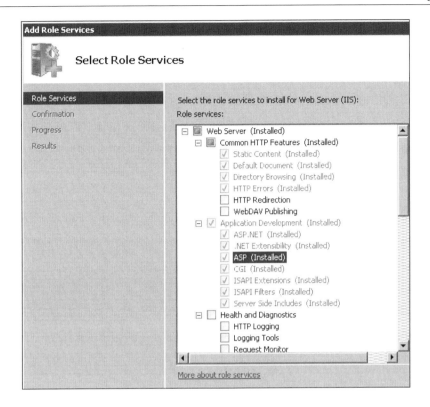

Writing the web service using ASP

Now we will start writing the web service. To do that, we will need to write some code. An artist needs a canvas to paint, and the canvas for programmers is the notepad. You may also use Notepad ++, Sublime Text, or your favorite editor. Click on **Start** and then type `Notepad`. In the open Notepad, type the following code:

```
<%
  Response.Write ("Hello, World!")
%>
```

The `<%` and `%>` tags indicate the opening and closing of the ASP code segment, `Response.Write` is a function that will output a value to whoever is calling the service, and `"Hello, World!"` is the string we want to output. This is just to test the service; we will change this later. Let's save this file at `C:\inetpub\wwwroot` as `genrand.asp`. Now open Chrome or any browser you have and type the following:

```
http://WEB-SERVER01/genrand.asp
```

This will output **"Hello, World!"** in the browser. Remember that you just called this service from the browser, so you will get the output there. If you called it from within a C++ application, Python script, or a terminal, you will get the result there. Let's refine the code, open our file again in Notepad, erase everything, and write the following code instead:

```
<%
Dim r
r = Rnd()
r = r * 100
r = Round(r)
Response.Write(r)
%>
```

Downloading the example code

You can download the example code files for all Packt books you have purchased from your account at http://www. packtpub.com. If you purchased this book elsewhere, you can visit http://www.packtpub. com/support and register to have the files e-mailed directly to you.

Save the file and run it again. You will get a random number. I got 71, and yours might be different. Try running the service again; you will get the exact same number. Why is that? The problem with generating random numbers with computers is that computers are predicable. They are machines that we program. Computers cannot just think of a number. It should come from somewhere, either from a time stamp or from an external value such as the weather temperature. If I asked you to think of a number, you will give me a different number every time. This is why hackers with experience can predict what the computer will do next if they could understand how the random generator algorithm is coded. The reason you are getting the same number is that every time you call this service, you initiate a new process that is not associated with the previous call. It happens that the first random number in my case is always 71. This is why you keep getting the same number every time you refresh the page, not so random. To create a real random number, we should seed it with something slightly unpredictable, and nothing is more unpredictable than nature. You could read different information on the weather such as wind velocity, temperature, and so on, and toss this data to create a random number. However, for the sake of this exercise, we will seed it with less predictable data, the time.

Let's open our file again and add the highlighted code shown as follows:

```
<%
Dim r
Randomize (Timer)
r = Rnd()
r = r * 100
r = Round(r)
Response.Write(r)
%>
```

Open your service again. Now you will start getting some different numbers. You can start adding more complexity to this service to generate even more random or even more unique numbers.

You might say this seems like a normal web page and that is true. However, instead of returning HTML content, this page returns a single number. So we computer scientists decided to give it another name, a web service, to differentiate it from the classical web page. For instance, consider the **Extensible Markup Language (XML)** and HTML languages. Both of them are markup languages at their cores. The difference is that HTML is a special case of XML with special tags that follow a standard. The **Geographic Markup Language (GML)** falls in the same category, a markup language with special geography tags. You can say that a web page is a special case of a web service that returns, well, a page.

Now that you know how a web service works, consider Twitter API, Facebook API, or ArcGIS API; all of these are web services exposed in the same way you just did. The only difference is that they follow a set of standards that make them universal and easier to consume.

Extensible Markup Language (XML) is a markup language that allows the use of tags to describe a document so it can be easily readable by both humans and machines.

A web page is a web service that uses HTTP as a medium and returns HTML content that the browser renders into visualized elements.

Web services' protocols

You may have noticed from the service you authored that it is up to you how you want to format the result. Imagine if each developer used his own format, it would be really difficult for other parties to consume your service without knowing its parameters. Therefore, a set of protocols were compiled and widely provided. We will talk about the importance of using a standard format and how much time it can save during integration.

The importance of a standard format

With the magnitude of flexibility in this age of information, we started to create so many diverse works. Isaac Newton started an excellent standard by which he could aggregate his work and present it properly to the world. He created **Calculus**, which is a unified language for the entire world; mathematicians adopted his approach of doing math because it was simple and effective. They came up with interesting theories based on that adaptation. Calculus was a standard, a protocol that has succeeded. Einstein wouldn't have invented the theory of relativity if it weren't for Newton. There are big companies creating standards in technology as well as organizations creating open standards so others can use them to invent something new, their next relativity theory. However, instead of following an existing standard, companies kept creating new standards, which led to duplicated rules and ways of doing work. This results in what I call "Standard Abundance", the reason why an application in iOS has to be completely rewritten for Android, Blackberry, and Windows Mobile in order to work. If the three smartphone makers were following one standard, we could have downloaded the same application from any smartphone, and any update on the application will be pushed to all smartphones. HTML is a great standard that thrived and succeeded. Although browsers tend to render HTML differently sometimes, it is still quite impressive that they all display a page that is relatively the same. If browsers were to follow their own standard, a dedicated website would need to be written for each browser; you may notice how the IE6 browser can demolish a website's look and feel because it doesn't support some of the new HTML standards, let alone a completely new standard.

The same problem applies to web plugins such as **Adobe Flash** and **Microsoft Silverlight**. 10 years ago, HTML was not equipped to be a multimedia platform. In fact, multimedia wasn't designed to be a part of the whole web ecosystem. So they created their own standard with their own programming languages as a browser plugin to do more on the Web. Flash entered the web market, and developers saw how easy it was to build a multimedia application and how user-friendly the applications looked. Companies liked flash so they used it in their websites, and action script developers, the scripting language for Adobe Flash, grew. Adobe Flash became de facto for a lot of websites on the Internet. Installing this web plugin was worth it to get all these rich features. Everything was quite rosy for Adobe until the introduction of HTML5 that supports basic multimedia features. Along the way, hackers managed to find flaws in Flash that made systems vulnerable. Companies started being skeptical about the use of Flash. With the introduction of the iPad and Steve Jobs' decision to not support Flash, things changed as if he somehow triggered an evolution, a tipping point, or the moment of critical mass as Malcolm Gladwell calls it. JavaScript, CSS3, and HTML5 developers started doing more. jQuery and Dojo libraries came into the picture, which allowed developers to perform more functionalities with fewer lines of code. Today HTML5 is getting better and better and the full standard will be released in 2014.

SOAP

SOAP is the first standard developed as a uniformed medium for web services; it uses XML as the communication protocol. Think of SOAP as a standard to format messages for both requests and responses transferred through web services. For instance, take our random number generator web service; we can make a small modification to comply with the SOAP standard by adding the following elements in the table:

Element	Description	Required?
Envelope	Identifies the XML document as a SOAP message.	Yes
Header	Contains header information.	No
Body	Contains call and response information.	Yes
Fault	Provides information about errors that occurred while processing the message.	No

So instead of returning just a number, you can return the random number with more useful information, which is the standard information that other applications can read, understand, and process uniformly. Here is a sample SOAP message for our random generator:

```
POST /InStock HTTP/1.1
Host: www.mywebsite.org
Content-Type: application/soap+xml; charset=utf-8
Content-Length: 299
SOAPAction: http://www.w3.org/2003/05/soap-envelope
<?xml version="1.0"?>
<soap:Envelope xmlns:soap="http://www.w3.org/2003/05/soap-envelope">
<soap:Header>
</soap:Header>
<soap:Body>
<m:GetRandomNumber xmlns:m="http://www.mywebsite.org/random">
      <m:Value>71</m:Value>
</m:GetRandomNumber>
</soap:Body>
</soap:Envelope>
```

Notice that the only value you will be using from that message is 71, and you will probably discard the entire message. However, it is a good practice to include it in this format for future use. Let's say you want to modify your web service to return the time stamp along with the random number. In our first example, you would probably add a separator next to the random number; however, using SOAP, you can just add another XML element and give it a proper name like <m:TimeStamp>31-May-2013 12:00AM</m:TimeStamp> that looks better than 71|31-May-2013 12:00AM. Or maybe instead of returning a single random number, if you want to return five random numbers, you can simply add five other <m:GetRandomNumber> elements as shown in the following code:

```
POST /InStock HTTP/1.1
Host: www.mywebsite.org
Content-Type: application/soap+xml; charset=utf-8
Content-Length: 299
SOAPAction: http://www.w3.org/2003/05/soap-envelope
<?xml version="1.0"?>
<soap:Envelope xmlns:soap="http://www.w3.org/2003/05/soap-envelope">
<soap:Header>
</soap:Header>
<soap:Body>

<m:TimeStamp>
31-May-2013 12:00AM
```

```
</m:TimeStamp>

<m:GetRandomNumber xmlns:m="http://www.mywebsite.org/random">
      <m:Value>71</m:Value>
</m:GetRandomNumber>

<m:GetRandomNumber xmlns:m="http://www.mywebsite.org/random">
      <m:Value>22</m:Value>
</m:GetRandomNumber>

<m:GetRandomNumber xmlns:m="http://www.mywebsite.org/random">
      <m:Value>41</m:Value>
</m:GetRandomNumber>

<m:GetRandomNumber xmlns:m="http://www.mywebsite.org/random">
      <m:Value>12</m:Value>
</m:GetRandomNumber>

<m:GetRandomNumber xmlns:m="http://www.mywebsite.org/random">
      <m:Value>88</m:Value>
</m:GetRandomNumber>

</soap:Body>
</soap:Envelope>
```

ArcGIS for desktop communicates with the server using SOAP over **Transmission Control Protocol (TCP)**. SOAP could work over other transfer protocols such as HTTP and **Simple Mail Transfer Protocol (SMTP)** as well; in our example, we have implemented it over HTTP. For additional security, you can implement it over the **Hyper Text Transfer Protocol Secure (HTTPS)** or on TCP for additional control.

REST

Although SOAP and REST usually are mentioned in the same context, they are completely different. Comparing SOAP to REST is like comparing a Dodge Challenger to a HEMI engine. A HEMI engine is a standard engine that can be used with almost any sports car. However, Challenger is a family of automobiles that includes many standardized parts, including an engine, which is not necessarily a HEMI engine. So in a nutshell, we could define **Representation State Transfer (REST)** as a complete architecture style (Challenger) that benchmarks the entire communication platform between a client and a server, including a standard format message (the engine), which can be anything, not necessarily XML as SOAP dictates.

Following are the elements that build up REST:

Element	Description
Client/server	Provides decoupled interfaces between the client and server, meaning client (regardless of what programming language is used) should implement an interface and the server should implement a different interface. This means when I change the client configuration such as changing its operating system or installing a service pack, it should not affect the server and vice versa.
Stateless	A state remembers some client variables, which can be used by the server to perform an action; for example, the Undo operation is a state-full action, and the server should save the previous state so it can roll back to that state. REST should be completely stateless, which means the server should not remember any state for the client because this makes the server dependent on the client.
Cacheable	Caching helps optimizing the communication by storing server responses on the client side and retrieving them locally instead of requesting them again. The server responses should be labeled as cacheable or not so the client knows when to cache a response and when to request new data.
Layered system	The client shouldn't explicitly know which server to connect to, which enables communication with an intermediate server, thus allowing room for load balancing.
Uniform interface	This is a uniform interface on both the client and server. This interface should carry a message with complete details on how to consume and process a request; for instance, the message should have enough information to tell the server how to parse the message.

An architecture that complies with all the five elements can be called a RESTful architecture. Clients consuming web services implemented on a proper RESTful environment can enjoy the privilege of scalability, and the server could be upgraded easily without the need for the client to worry about it. A good example is my experience with the Twitter REST API back in 2009 when Twitter was just establishing their API. I started building a lot of applications using the Twitter API, adding some geographical flavor to Twitter. One such application was **EarthTwit** where a user could sign into Twitter from **Google Earth** and retrieve all his followers and friends, geocode their location using **Google Geocoder**, then project them onto Google Earth. A user could tweet from EarthTwit, and she/he could also share a location from Google Earth to Twitter. One day, my users started to complain that EarthTwit was not working; the followers were not displayed on Google Earth. After some time, I discovered that Twitter had upgraded their API to a newer version and all my applications, including EarthTwit, were bugged.

I had to change the entire code to make it work with the new API. If Twitter had used a RESTful paradigm, my applications would have worked after the upgrade. Fortunately, ArcGIS for Server is a RESTful architecture, and it also supports the SOAP standard.

The Web server

A web service is hosted on a Web server, which is a solution that serves clients over the Web. There is a lot of Web server software available in the market that is free, open source, and commercial. These range from lightweight home use that supports a few requests to those designed to support millions of requests.

GIS services

Now that we know how web services work, it is time to get back to the Server. A GIS service is a web service, which has a geographic element. Many standards for GIS service were developed and are widely implemented; in this chapter, we will discuss and author **Esri map services** and some of the **Open Geospatial Consortium (OGC)** services.

Map services

In GIS, we usually deal with maps. Esri map services are GIS services that handle operations on a geographical map. You can publish a map as a map service and consume this service from any client that supports this type of service. Map services are widely used and are famous for their simplicity and portability. The map services authoring tool for Server is ArcGIS for Desktop; hereafter, it is called Desktop. You cannot create a map service without this product, Desktop doesn't have to be installed on the same machine as your Server — as long as they are on the same network, you are good.

Connecting to the Server site

To publish our map, we first need to connect to the Server site we created in the previous chapter. Whether you followed the Express or Advanced installation track, you should have a Server site with one or more machines and perhaps a Web server. If you remember, in the previous chapter, we discussed how the Server site is hosted on a Web server. We also said that with each GIS server, Esri installs a hidden built-in Web server running on port 6080. We created a dedicated Web server in the Production track to host the Server site. We also illustrated how the server site could be accessed by either the built-in Web Server or the dedicated Web server.

To access the Server site, we can access the built-in web servers in GIS servers by connecting to it. To do so, I have GIS-SERVER01 and GIS-SERVER02, so any of the two URLs `http://GIS-SERVER01:6080/` or `http://GIS-SERVER02:6080/` will work fine. If you have set up a dedicated Web server with the Production Track, you may use it for the connection as well, thus giving you high availability. Mind that you should use a web adaptor with administrator access enabled. We have created the `waadmin` credential on WEB-SERVER01 in the previous chapter that allows us to do that. The URL to establish the connection will look like `http://WEB-SERVER01/waadmin/`.

Let us create a connection so we can start publishing map services; this task requires ArcGIS for Desktop. Log into a machine with a Desktop installation and open ArcCatalog. We will call this machine the **Publisher** machine; you may install Desktop on one of your GIS servers if you want to. From the **Catalog Tree**, expand the **GIS Servers** node and double-click on **Add ArcGIS Server**. In the **Add ArcGIS Server** form, you will have three options. The first one uses GIS services, which is a read-only connection. You probably want to create this connection for your public users to only consume the services. The third option, Administer GIS server, is a connection that allows you to manage the Server site, so you can create and delete services using this option. This is similar to the ArcGIS Server Manager Web interface that can be accessed from `http://GIS-SERVER01:6080/arcgis/manager`. The second option, Publish GIS services, is the one we will be selecting is a connection that will allow you to publish services. Since this involves changing the site configuration, we will need to enter the primary administrator's username and password to create this connection. The following table gives us the reference list of the Server site connections that you can establish. Click on **Next**.

 If you are using ArcGIS 10, you will get two options instead of three. In this case, you may choose the Manage GIS Services option.

Connection type	Description
User	A connection that allows a basic read-only access to site services. This doesn't require credentials unless the Server site is set up with security.
Publisher	A connection that allows for publishing a service. This requires credentials to create the connection.
Admin	A connection with elevated privileges, which allows for managing the services in the Site.

In the next form, we will enter the parameters required to create the publisher connection. In the **Server URL** field, type the Server site URL. As discussed earlier, it could be one of your GIS-Servers running on port 6080 or your dedicated Web server. If you have installed a Web Adaptor, you can use GIS-SERVER01. So it will be `http://GIS-SERVER01:6080/arcgis/`. The default **Server Type** should be **ArcGIS Server**; there is another option for Spatial Data Server, an older version that Esri will retire soon. We will not be using this option in this book. Enter the site's primary administrator account authentication in the **User Name** and **Password** fields and then click on **Finish** to create your connection.

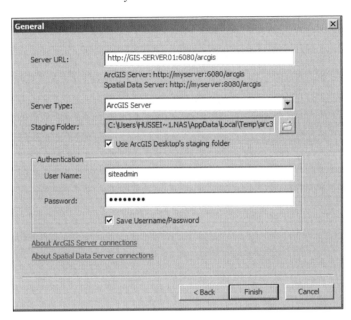

Rename the connection to `Publisher@GIS-Server01`. This connection you just created will be used to publish web services for which we will require ArcMap to author. Note that if GIS-SERVER01 is down for any reason, be it maintenance or a temporary restart, you will not be able to establish the Server site connection. Even if your Server site has other GIS servers, they will not take over this connection because we have physically hard wired the connection to one of them only.

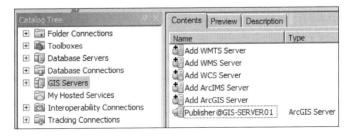

To establish a secure and more managed Server site connection, you can use a dedicated Web server. In the **General** form, enter `http://WEB-SERVER01/waadmin/` in the server URL field and the primary site administrator credentials in the **User Name** and **Password** fields. Then click on **Finish** and rename the connection to `Publisher@WEB-SERVER01`.

Best practice

Avoid establishing Server site connections through GIS servers; instead, use a dedicated Web server whenever applicable to maintain a highly available connection.

TO-DO

Create the following two connections: Admin@WEB-SERVER01 that has administration privileges and User@WEB-SERVER01 that is a read-only connection. Mind that a user connection does not require credentials.

Disabling automatic data copying

ArcGIS for Server, by default, tries to copy the service data when the data source is not registered. This can cause problems with large data in Version 10.1, so Esri added the option to disable automatic data copying in Version 10.2. It is recommended that you disable the automatic data copying configuration from your Server site. To log in to the **ArcGIS Server Manager** and go to **Site**, from the left pane click on **Data Store**, click on **Setting** and uncheck **Allow data to be copied to the site when publishing services**, and then click on **Save**.

Authoring map services with file geodatabase

Now that we have created a publisher connection, we will use it to send our map to the Server site in order to create a map service. Any map service requires connecting to a geodatabase, which stores the map data. In this chapter, we will author our first Map Service with a sample data, which is located locally on the Server on a file geodatabase. You can download the `LandParcels.gdb` geodatabase from the book's project page at `www.packtpub.com` and extract it to the `C:` drive.

The geodatabase in this example includes a LandParcels feature class. To author map services, we will need ArcGIS for Desktop, specifically ArcMap. In the previous chapter, we installed the Server successfully, so I will be using the same machine names for demonstration purposes.

Log in to your publisher machine again and launch ArcMap; once ArcMap is started, click on **Add Data** to open the **Add Data** dialog. Browse to C:\AGSA\Data\ LandParcels.gdb, double-click on the geodatabase to open it, and then double click on the LandParcels feature class to add it to the map.

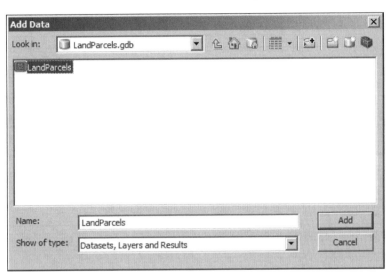

There is a lot of work to be done in ArcMap in order to author a good presentable map and eventually publish it as a map service. There are plenty of tips and best practices to author an efficient map to result in an optimized map service, which will be explained in *Chapter 5, Optimizing GIS Services*. The result of adding the LandParcels feature class doesn't look as attractive as you might want, so we will add some basic symbology and labeling work to create a good map. Your skills in ArcMap will come in handy now.

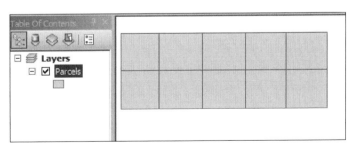

Double click on the layer **Parcels** and select the **Symbology** tab. Click on **Categories** and then from the **Value Field** drop-down list, select **CATEGORY** and click on **Add All Values** to add all the categories of symbology to the layer.

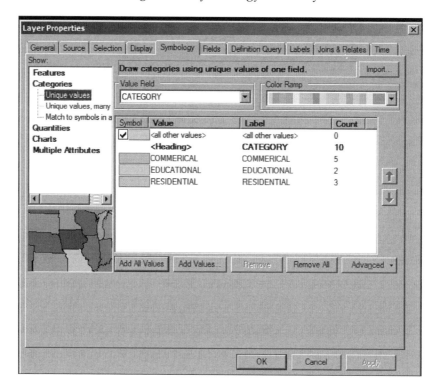

Click on the **Labels** tab. Check the **Label** features in this layer option and then from the **Label Field**, select **PARCELNO** and click on **OK**.

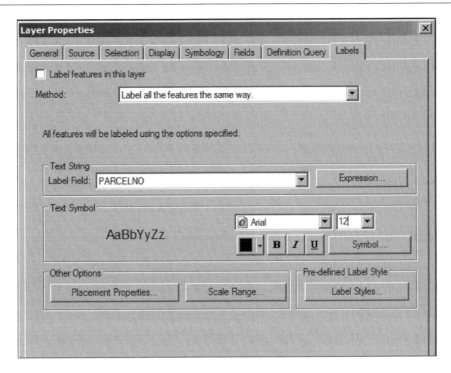

You should now see your parcels colored and labeled on the map as shown in the following screenshot:

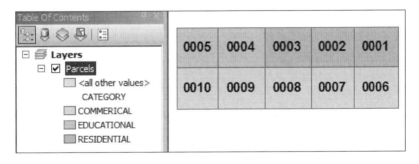

Now that the map is complete, it is ready to be published; however, first we need to save this document. Click on **Save**, select `C:\AGSA\Documents`, and name it `Parcels_FGDB.mxd`. To publish the service, perform the following steps:

1. From the **File** menu, point to **Share As** and then click on **Service**.

2. From the new form that has popped up, select the **Publish a Service** option and click on **Next**.

3. From the drop-down list, select the **Publisher@GIS-SERVER01** connection, which is the Server site connection we created earlier, and wait until a connection is established. Note that the server GIS-SERVER01 should be up and running for the connection to get established.

4. In the **Service Name** field type `Parcels_FGDB` so we know that this service is using a file geodatabase. Then click on **Next**.

5. ArcGIS for Server allows you to group your services into folders so they become easily manageable. You also get extra benefit by adding extra security at the folder level as well. For now, just choose the default root folder and click on **Continue**.

6. Here is where the fun begins. There are a lot of different settings and configurations that you can apply to your map service; however, we will just publish the map service as is for now without changing any parameters. Don't worry, in the upcoming chapters, you will understand and will start tweaking all these options as you see fit. At one point, you will even create a template of your preferred configuration and import them to any newly created map service.

7. Click on **Analyse**. This will run some analysis on your map. There are warnings that we will ignore for now and fix later. There is one warning however that I want you to pay attention to, which is shown in the following table:

Severity	Status	Code	Description	Name	Type	Data frame
High	Unresolved	24011	Layer's data source is not registered with the server and data will be copied to the server.	Parcels	Layer	Layers

To explain this message, we should first understand how the Server works. In an ideal world, a client requests a map service. Let's say the clients wants to zoom in to a particular extent of a map. There is a Web server that accepts the client's request and forwards it to the GIS server, subject to availability and load. The target GIS server then connects to the map service's data source, calculates the new extent, and returns the data in that extent. At this stage, the data source should be accessible by the GIS server; as a matter of fact, all GIS servers should have access to the data source. In our case, the data source is a local file geodatabase located on GIS-SERVER01. By default, GIS-SERVER01 has access to it because it is located on the same machine. But what happens if you add another GIS server to your Server site? Then, GIS-SERVER02 will not be able to connect to the data source because it is not available locally or remotely. Server gives you a quick solution to that by copying the entire geodatabase to each GIS server and gives pop-up messages as a warning. The downside is that the process takes a lot of time in publishing and might cause ArcMap to crash. Moreover, if you constantly update your geodatabase, you will have inconsistent data. To solve that, we need to register the data source with the Server site so all GIS servers point to one data source instead of copies. This will be covered in the coming pages. However, for now, we will just publish the map service with the default configuration as is. We will allow the data to be copied to the GIS server. The `LandParcels` feature class has only few features, hence the copying process shouldn't take long. Click on **Publish** to upload the data and publish the map service.

During the process of copying a data source to the server process, ArcMap might crash as it runs out of memory. In this case, simply restart the publishing process.

Registering the data source

Copying data source to the GIS servers makes sense when your ArcGIS for Server is running on the cloud. Since it is inefficient for the cloud GIS servers to connect to your local data source, sending a copy to the cloud is more effective so that the cloud GIS servers to crunch it up locally. Otherwise, if all your Server setup is on a local network, you are better off registering the data source.

 Best practice
Always register any new data source if your Server site is on the same network as the geodatabase.

Registering a folder

Registering a folder that contains a personal or file geodatabase will make it available for all GIS servers on the Server site. Therefore, instead of copying the data source to all GIS servers, Server will simply connect to the registered folder. To do that, we first need to share our geodatabase so it could be accessible from multiple locations. Our database should be in a location that is highly available, a data server perhaps or a NAS box. For this exercise, we will use the WEB-SERVER01 as the geodatabase repository as we have done with the Production Installation Track when we used it as a configuration store.

 If you have followed the Testing Installation Track, you may skip this topic.

Go ahead and copy the **LandParcels** geodatabase to the WEB-SERVER01 on the `C:\AGSA\Data\` and create the folder if it is not there. Next, we need to share the `C:\AGSA\Data\` folder, right-click on the `Data` folder and click on **Properties**. Activate the **Share** tab and click on **Share type** in the ArcGIS for Server user account that you used for installing `GIS\arcgis.server` or `agsServer`, depending on your configuration. Click on **Add**, this will give you access to GIS servers that will have access to this folder. Remember, if you use a dedicated publisher machine, you need to login to that machine using the `GIS\arcgis.server` domain name. Click on **Share**. Now, you should be able to access the following geodatabase folder `\\WEB-SERVER01\Data`.

Best practice

If you are planning to use a file or personal geodatabase, it is recommended to have it hosted on a Network Array Storage or a dedicated data server.

Now, log in to the ArcGIS Server Manager from Chrome using the URL `http://GIS-SERVER01:6080/arcgis/manger` or `http://WEB-SERVER01/waadmin` if you have installed the Web Adaptor, as discussed in the previous chapter. We also bookmarked the page so you can go back to it easily from Chrome. Enter the primary administrator account credentials to log in and and click on **Site**. From the left pane, select **Data Store** and then click on the **Register Folder** button. From the **Register Folder** form, type `GeoDB` in the **Name** field. The **Publisher Folder Path** is the path where your geodatabase is located; mine is `\\WEB-SERVER01\Data\`. Optionally, you can specify the publisher hostname, which is the machine you are publishing the map from. I'm using one of the GIS servers as a publisher machine. This saves time, but of course, you might want to dedicate a separate machine for publishing if you are planning to fit in a workflow. Click on **Create**.

If you get an error that means the ArcGIS Server account cannot access that folder, make sure the right privileges are set accordingly. Click on **Validate All** to validate all the data stores. You should see your folder added and validated.

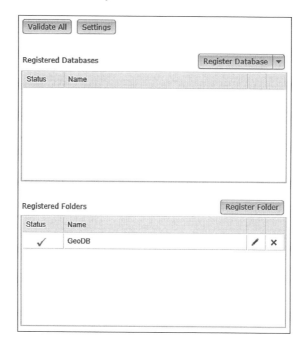

To publish a map with a registered geodatabase, you need to add the geodatabase from the ArcMap by connecting to the shared folder using the UNC path, \\WEB-SERVER01\Data\. This is the only way you will be able to register the database. Let us publish a second map service this time with a registered data source:

1. Open ArcMap and click on **Add Data**.

2. Click on the **Connect to Folder** icon and type in \\WEB-SERVER01\Data\.

3. In the folder field, browse to your LandParcels feature class and click on **Add**.

4. Follow the same steps for the symbology as well as labeling and publishing the map service. Name the service Parcels_FGDB_R.

Note that the warning for registering the database has disappeared. This design might work fine for small read-only geodatabases. However, as your database gets larger and more editing is performed on this shared geodatabase, your performance will start to slow down. There have also been incidents where users get inconsistent results when editing file geodatabases on shared folders. That is why it is recommended to move to an enterprise geodatabase that can handle sophisticated networking and large number of edits.

Registering with an enterprise geodatabase

An enterprise geodatabase or Esri **Spatial Database Engine** (**SDE**) was designed to allow clients the ability to provide high-speed access to the geodatabase through sophisticated networking. That is the beauty of SDE. Place your database on a powerful server and let users access it. There is a catch here though, for clients to be able to connect successfully to the enterprise server hosting the database, the connecting machine (in our case, this is usually the GIS server) should have the necessary client database binary that permits this connection, and this binary should match ArcGIS for Server architecture. For instance, Server cannot use a 32-bit Oracle database client to connect to the geodatabase because Server is a 64-bit software. So, you need to install a 64-bit Oracle database client on the GIS servers. Not only do you need to install the right database client on all your GIS servers, but you also have to make sure they all use the same connection parameters, same database server name, IP address, port, credentials, and SDE version. Only when all these are identical and duplicated on all GIS servers will you be able to register your enterprise geodatabase.

If you have a working SDE, you should follow this step before authoring your SDE map service. My SDE runs SQL Server Express 2008 R2 64 bit on a workstation named SDE-SERVER01. I have also installed the client SQL Server Express 64 bit on my GIS servers: GIS-SERVER01 and GIS-SERVER02. So, they can use it to establish the connection. I suggest you do the same with your database client, install the same client on all your GIS servers. After you complete the installation, let us create an SDE connection to SDE-SERVER01. The configuration of that connection will be saved in a .sde file, which we will use to register the SDE database. Open **ArcCatalog** and go to **Database Connections** and double-click on **Add Database Connection**. From the **Database Platform** drop-down list, select **SQL Server type** in the instance; mine is SDESQLExpress. Click on **Connect**. Rename the connection in this format: User@CONNECTION-VERSION. Hence, mine will look like SDE@ SDESQLExpress-DEFAULT, which indicates that it is connecting to the SQL server connection using SDE as the user and SDE.DEFAULT as the default version. Double-click on the connection to make sure you can connect successfully; if that worked, you will find the connection file on your local settings because connection files are available per user. You will find them in the following path: C:\Users\ username\AppData\Roaming\ESRI\Desktop10.x\ArcCatalog. Make a copy of that file on C:\AGSA\Connections. We are now ready to register the data source.

Depending on your enterprise database, these steps may differ slightly. But all will lead to the connection file that we will use to register the data source.

From the same machine, you configured your SDE connection. Fire up Chrome and launch ArcGIS for Server Manager, then perform the following:

1. Go to the Site.
2. From the left pane, select **Data Store** and then click on the **Register Database** button.
3. Click on **Browse** to select your `.sde` connection file that you created earlier on `C:\AGSA\Connections`.
4. Make sure the **Match Publisher** connection is checked so that we use the same connection parameters.
5. Click on **Register**.

This will verify that this SDE connection can be established from all your GIS servers. If this succeeded, it means your GIS servers can successfully connect to this data source. If, however, you are prompted with an error, one of your GIS servers have failed to connect to this database using these parameters. So, you can go to each GIS server to make sure the database client is installed and you can connect to your database. In my case, it is SQL Server Express 2008 R2 64 bit. It should be 64 bit though, because Server is built on a 64-bit architecture.

It is not required to install ArcGIS for Desktop on your GIS servers to establish an SDE connection. The database client is the most important element. The rest of the necessary drivers to establish an SDE connection is installed by ArcGIS for Server.

Authoring map service with enterprise geodatabase

Having an enterprise geodatabase running behind is the most stable approach for authoring map services. If you are planning to serve many users you should consider using SDE map services, and you don't necessarily require a commercial DBMS product if you don't have the budget for one. You can go with PostgreSQL or SQL Server Express as ArcGIS for Server supports both.

Best practice

It is recommended to register your enterprise geodatabase as a data source before continuing with this exercise. Avoid the use of the copy to Server option when you have an enterprise geodatabase.

In registering an enterprise geodatabase topic, we created an enterprise connection. Now, we will use that connection to add data to ArcMap from the database, do some work on the map, and publish the map as a map service. We will also save this document so we can update it later if required. From the same machine that you created the SDE connection, launch ArcMap and follow the given steps:

1. Click on **Add Data**.

2. Go to database connection, select **SDE@SDESQLExpress-DEFAULT**, select the **LandParcels** feature class, and follow the same steps to do the symbology work, as we did in the previous topic.

3. Finally, save the map document to C:\AGSA\Documents\Parcels_SDE.mxd.

 The steps to publish the service are generic and independent of the database.

4. From the **File** menu, point to **Share As**, click on **Service**, select the **Publish a Service** option, and click on **Next**.

5. From the drop-down list, select either **Publisher@GIS-SERVER01** or **Publisher@WEB-SERVER01** connection and wait until a connection is established.

6. In the **Service Name** field, type Parcels_SDE so we know that this service is using an enterprise geodatabase.

7. Click on **Next**.

8. Then click on **Analyse** to analyze the map.

You might receive a warning, but the key point is to make sure that your SDE connection is registered so the server doesn't have to copy the data to GIS servers. You have completed authoring an SDE map service. You might not be comfortable with users connecting as the SDE user. After all, the SDE user has full control over the geodatabase and it is not good practice to give end users this privilege. It might be a good idea to create a dedicated user in your DBMS, let's call it AGSSERVER, with read-only privileges on the data you are using. This way, you will be able to monitor connections coming from Server by filtering it for AGSSERVER. In that case, you have to create a new SDE connection AGSSERVER@SDESQLExpress-DEFAULT from ArcCatalog. Since this is a new connection, you have to register a new database on Server. You can do that by taking the .sde connection file and registering and adding it to the data source from the Manager as explained earlier.

SDE connections are tricky. You must register a new data source for every connection parameter that differs. For instance, if you want to create another SDE connection that points to another version or connects using another user, you should create a new connection and register that particular connection .sde file separately.

Offline authoring and publishing

There will be cases in which your publishers and map authors do not have direct access to the server—perhaps they are just in another office, a firewall option prevents them from connecting, or maybe the network is down. ArcGIS for Server gives you the ability to author a map offline, save it into a service definition .sd file, and publish the service using this file. The file can be sent in an e-mail or transferred in a USB thumb drive. So, let us see how we could do this:

1. Open your **Parcels** document, point to **File**, then **Share As**, and then select **Service**.

2. From the **Share As** service form, select the **Save a service definition** file and then click on **Next**.

3. From the **Save a Service Definition** form, select the **No available** connection option.

4. Check the **Include data in the sd file** option so the data will be fused in the file, type Parcels_from_sd into the **Service Name** field, click on **Next**, and then select where you want to save your file.

5. Let us save it in C:\AGSA\ServiceDefinitions. Click on **Continue** and then click the **Stage** button to save the .sd file.

Now we have to publish the map service using this file. Go and log in to one of your GIS servers. Log in to the ArcGIS Server Manager and you will see a **Publish Service** button. Click on it and browse for your .sd file, making sure you have copied it from the publisher machine. It shouldn't be that big; in our case, it is less than 1 MB. After you select the file, click on **Next**. Leave everything to the default settings and just click on **Next** and then **Publish**.

Protocols enabled for map services

ArcGIS for Server enables both SOAP and REST for any published map service. Not only does the server permit you to use both protocols on the same map service, but it also gives you the luxury to enable **Open Geospatial Consortium (OGC)** standards. Up until now, no product could give you all these functionalities. It shows that Esri is investing well into this technology and draws a clear strategic path that it is planning to support Server for years to come. Later in this chapter, we will briefly explain how to consume SOAP, REST, and WMS services from different clients; however, *Chapter 3, Consuming GIS Services*, will discuss richly how to consume different types of map services from different clients.

 By default, ArcGIS for Server enables both REST and SOAP access for any published map service.

OGC services

Map services are Web services standardized by Esri, and not all clients know how to consume them. So, if you published your services as Esri map services, you will limit your users to this standard. There are, however, other standards for Web services that serve GIS content and luckily, ArcGIS for Server allows you to enable these standards on your services easily. Among them are OGC standards. These standards have been designed to support different needs for each Web service. As we have discussed in *The importance of a standard format* section, standards were created to make things blend within a big homogenous ecosystem. There are many OGC web services and the following table explains some of the widely used ones. In this chapter, we will discuss how to publish a Web map service.

OGC service	Description
WMS	**Web map service (WMS)** is a basic service that returns images only. No information is included with the image.
WFS	**Web feature service (WFS)** is a rich service that returns full XML data of each element in the map.
WPS	**Web processing service (WPS)** is a geoprocessing service that permits executing a geocode command and returns the result.

Authoring WMS services

ArcGIS for Server supports publishing a WMS service along with other OGC services. In fact, the thing that made Server one of the popular map publishing solutions is its ability to adhere to open standards, which makes it one of the top used solutions for organizations. WMS is a good option if you want to give your client a flavor of your maps, but without them querying and poking around its attributes, you want them only to see a base image map. To publish a WMS service, we just have to enable the WMS capability while publishing the map from ArcMap. Let us open one of the map documents that we saved in the previous exercises in the C:\AGSA\Documents folder. You can either choose Parcels_FGDB.mxd or Parcels_SDE.mxd, and either will work. I will select the SDE as it is the most stable one because it uses an enterprise geodatabase, which can handle the incoming connections from the WMS. After ArcMap opens, go to **File** | **Share As**, then click on **Service** then select the **Publish a Service** option, and click on **Next**. From the drop-down list, select the **Publisher@GIS-SERVER01** connection and wait until a connection is established. In the **Service Name** field type Parcels_SDE_WMS; if you have selected **FGDB**, type Parcels_FGDB_WMS instead, so you know that this service is using a file geodatabase and it is published as a WMS service. Click on **Next**.

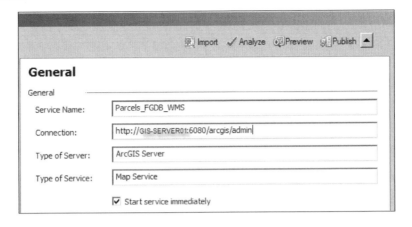

From the left pane, click on **Capabilities**. You will see all the different standards that you can enable on your service. Check **WMS**. After that, a new item will be added under **Capabilities**. Select **WMS**. Note that **REST URL** is disabled; this is because WMS only supports SOAP and it was not designed for large architecture like REST. Make sure the **Enter service properties below** option is selected and enter the metadata for the WMS service so clients can utilize this information when consuming your service. Finally, enable **Use layer names** from the map document so the service inherits the same layer naming conventions as your map document. Click on **Publish** to finally publish your map service.

Authoring WFS services

WMS is a 15 year old standard, yet it is still used by many clients for its simplicity. However, with the recent information explosion, the raw image returned by the WMS is not enough for analysis. The result should carry information and metadata that helps define its components and permits users to spatially analyze its elements. That is why OGC came up with a better standard, WFS. Instead of returning an image, the map is broken down into overlaid features that are then drawn by the client. There is also an option that allows the map service to be published as transactions, WFS (WFS-T). This option permits adding, deleting, and updating features on the service. ArcGIS has long used the concept of features in its software to support this new standard. To publish a WFS service, follow the same steps as mentioned in the *Authoring WMS Services* section. Give your service the name `Parcels_SDE_WFS`, or if you have selected **FGDB**, type `Parcels_FGDB_WFS`. Activate the WFS capability and expand the WFS option. Fill in the metadata of the service. We will not enable editing on the service for the time being, so make sure **Enable transactions** is unchecked. Click on **Publish**.

Note that we have created two dedicated services for each OGC standard, one for WMS and another for WFS. We could also create one map service with the two capabilities; this will save us time by maintaining only one service instead of two. However, you will find instances where you need to create multiple map services because you want to control what users can access and set up security for each service. Assume that you enabled WMS and WFS-T on a map service, you shared the WMS SOAP link to a user (Alice) who is supposed to only consume the images. You sent the WFS SOAP link to another user (Bob) who is a publisher. Although Alice has only the WMS link, she can easily construct the WFS link as it is essentially the same service with the same name. Moreover, any security privileges given to Alice have been given to Bob so both can access the service. This means that Alice will gain access to the WFS-T link, giving her elevated privileges to edit the data. On the other hand, if we created two map services, we could assign Bob to the WFS-T service and Alice to the WMS service. This way, Alice cannot access Bob's service. We will discuss this in detail in *Chapter 4, Planning and Designing GIS Services*, and *Chapter 7, Securing ArcGIS for Server*.

Best practice

Multiple capabilities can be enabled for a given map service. However, these have to be planned and carefully selected to avoid a flaw.

Geoprocessing services

Geoprocessing operation is an operation that works on spatial data. For example, buffering geoprocessing service takes a point and returns all features within a specified radius. Before geoprocessing, developers used to write customized tools to do simple tasks such as buffering, updating mass attribute, and clipping an area. When Esri created the model builder, users were able to mash up built-in tools to create **models**. These models can be used again as a submodel in an even bigger model. This remained the strategy until the release of ArcGIS for Server in 2006, which gave power to do that processing over services. Clients were able to call geoprocessing services right from their thin clients and return the results. Since then Esri has been moving its entire native functions into models, which can be eventually moved into services. Esri geoprocessing services can also be published as the WPS OGC standard to open up room for more clients to consume geoprocessing services created by Server. Esri began moving ArcGIS native operations into geoprocessing tools. This made it easier for end users to tap into the power of ArcGIS and reuse these tools to their advantage.

Testing the GIS services

We have learned how to author services in ArcGIS for Server. However, we still do not know how to consume these services. There are plenty of ways to use these ripe services in clients for visualization, analysis, and editing. We will discuss this thoroughly in the next chapter. Meanwhile we will test if our services work by using ArcMap. First, we need to create a user connection. This is a good chance to check if you did your TO-DO exercise right. The reason we are using a user connection is that end users should consume services at read-only privileges. If you connect to a map service using a publisher or an admin connection, the users will be prompted with a credential box. You have not only prevented them from consuming the service but also exposed your Server site for a potential brute force attack. A chain is only as strong as its weakest link.

Best practice

If you are planning to test a map service or want to use it for analysis or visualization, or perhaps share it with other users, you should always connect using a user connection that is set to use the GIS service only.

Open **ArcCatalog** and from the **Catalog Tree**, expand **GIS Servers**. Double-click on **Add ArcGIS Server** and select the **Use GIS services** option, and click on **Next**. In the **Server URL** field, type in your Server site URL. If you are using a dedicated Web server, as we set up one in the previous chapter, it is better to use that. If you don't have one, you can use one of the built-in Web servers in any of your GIS servers at `http://GIS-SERVER01:6080/arcgis`. However, you have to take into consideration that accessing this needs an access to port `6080`. So, if the user is behind a firewall, you need to enable it. You won't have this problem with a dedicated Web server because you will be running on the default port `80`. I will use the Web server at the URL `http://WEB-SERVER01/wa/`. Note that I have used the `wa` adaptor instead of the `waadmin`. We do not want our users to have access to the administrators' panel through an elevated web adaptor. Next, leave the **Authentication** boxes empty as we have not yet set up the security on our services, and click on **Finish**.

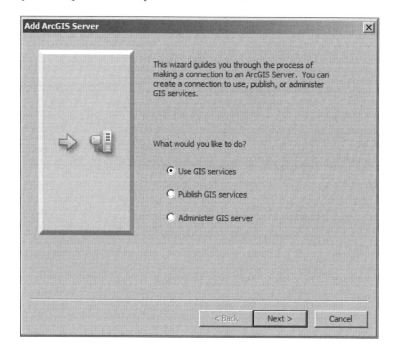

You will see your connection created; rename the connection to `User@WEB-SERVER01` or `User@GIS-SERVER01`, depending on which server you are connected to.

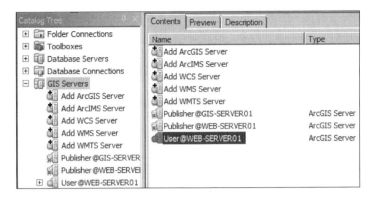

Double-click on your connection. You should start seeing the services you have authored listed. Click on one of them and select the **Preview** tab to see its content. This is one of the easiest ways to see if your services are working. However, we want to test it from ArcMap, so let us create a layer file. From **ArcCatalog**, right-click on the service **Parcles_FGDB** and select **Create Layer**. Save the layer file to `C:\AGSA\Layers` and name it `Parcels_FGDB.lyr`. This will create a layer file with the necessary parameters to consume this service from any ArcGIS for Desktop client in the local area network, which has the Web server or the GIS server in it. Close **ArcCatalog**. Fire up ArcMap, click on **Add Data**, navigate to the folder `C:\AGSA\Layers`, and select the layer file you just saved. Note that ArcMap tries to connect using the user connection stored in the layer file and then projects the data automatically. A good thing to note here is that when a map service is added to ArcMap, some of the options are locked, which restricts the user from changing it, thus giving the publisher the control over how a particular service should look. For example, if you double-click on the layer, you will see most of the options are grayed out, locking the layer from modification.

I remember one of my clients had an interesting requirement that made use of this particular feature in ArcGIS for Server. The client has a feature class that contained land information of the country. The users were using this feature class to zoom in to the particular land in order to work on a project. However, the client did not want this feature class exposed to users for exporting, clipping, or even printing on large scales, especially because this includes some sensitive information. So, I suggested revoking all users' read/write privileges on that feature class and allowing read-only access to the ArcGIS for Server user. I then asked them to create a map document, add the feature class, and set the scale to 2,000, on which the users usually work. The users shouldn't peek into the data above the scale of 2,000. So, we published the new map service, created a user connection to Server, created a layer file from the map service, and shared it with all the users. The users were able to search and zoom in to the project and work with the land information only at a scale of 2,000. They could not change this scale because it was set by the publisher, and they can't export or clip the data; nevertheless, they still satisfied the client's requirement.

Summary

In this chapter, you learned the concept behind a Web service. You managed to author your own service from scratch. That was necessary to understand the Web services protocols. Once you got the idea of Web services, we dived into the GIS services, which were basically Web services with a geographic dimension. You learned how to author and publish GIS services while enabling the widely available standards so that they can be consumed by various GIS clients. In the next chapter, we will discuss how to consume the GIS services for visualization, analysis, and editing.

3
Consuming GIS Services

In *Chapter 2, Authoring Web Services*, we learned about the concept of web services. We glanced at their types and managed to author basic GIS services. It was a slightly theoretical chapter with some definitions that were necessary to equip you with the basics to kick-start this book. In this chapter, we will learn how to consume and interact with the services we authored; after all, what is the use of these services if we don't know how to use them?

The real power of Server will start to surface in this chapter. You will see how your data can be put to good use, and how sharing it can open up a whole new dimension for potential analysis. You will be surprised to see how your data can be used in conjunction with others' data, if published on your intranet or publicly. There are a lot of people with great ideas out there who would love to have access to your data to create useful applications. You can even reach a stage where it is possible to sell your services per usage. Similarly, you can consume other services and add them to your data. For instance, a government could have a Server installation where all government entities can supply secured services of its data to this centralized ArcGIS for Server installation. Imagine a scenario where the traffic department is monitoring the flow of traffic in the city with a real-time map service layer with **Geographical Rich Site Summary (GeoRSS)** enabled. There is a traffic jam on one of the roads. A traffic police officer guesses that it is probably an accident, so he adds the recent accidents layer, also real time, to overlay it with the traffic layer. He notes that there are no accidents on that road so he adds the incidents layer to check the recent incidents in the area. The incidents layer shows a water leak from a main pipe on that road causing vehicles to slow down, therefore creating congestion.

 GeoRSS is a standard for encoding locations into a real-time web feed.

This chapter is divided into three main sections, the first section, *Using GIS services for visualization*, is where you will learn how to present your data and mash different services together to create rich maps that you can share easily or put onto your website or blog. The second section, *Using GIS services for editing*, is the editing part. It allows you to use featured services to edit your data and add new records to your geodatabase; this is very useful for you if you have people on the field with mobile devices into which they can feed in data directly from the field. The final section, *Using GIS services for analysis*, highlights the analysis part and discusses how to analyze data in order to find useful patterns that help answer questions.

I can promise you this chapter will be interesting and full of practical exercises. You can even start the book with this chapter if you are already comfortable with your ArcGIS for Server setup and already know how to create GIS services.

Before you start

There are a few things we have to do before we go into the fun part of putting your map services to use.

Getting the map service URL

To consume the services, we first need to get a unique pointer to the service. There is a dedicated URL for each standard that the map service supports. For instance, to consume the map service over SOAP, you will need a SOAP URL. This applies to REST and all OGC standards where each end point returns different results, as seen in *Chapter 2, Authoring Web Services*. We have shown that Server enables both REST and SOAP protocols on any published map service by default, and we have learned how to enable other standards such as WMS on the GIS service. To get the URL, we need to log in to ArcGIS for Server Manager; go ahead and click on the Manager bookmark you saved earlier. In case you didn't bookmark Manager, you can access it from here: `http://GIS-SERVER01:6080/arcgis/manager`. Use the credentials for the primary administrator account. You will see the list of services that you have published. Scroll to `Parcels_FGDB` and click on it to view its details. From the left-hand pane, click on **Capabilities** to view the supported protocols published for this map service, and then select **Mapping (always enabled)**. It should be activated by default, but just in case, this will list the default supported protocols SOAP and REST as shown in the following screenshot:

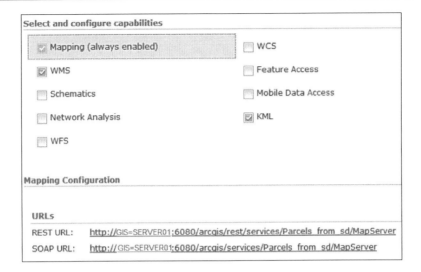

The URL `http://GIS-SERVER01:6080/arcgis/rest/services/Parcels_FGDB /` `MapServer` points to the map service using the REST protocol; we will use these links in our future exercises.

Best practice

This URL points to one of the physical GIS servers directly, so if this server is down for some reason, you will not be able to access the service even if you have another GIS server joined to the site. Therefore, it is recommended that you convert this URL to the Web Adaptor version through your dedicated Web server; refer to *Chapter 1, Best Practices for Installing ArcGIS for Server*, for more details.

If, however, you published one of your map services as an OGC, like we did back in *Chapter 2, Authoring Web Services*, and you want to get the WMS link, you have to select the **WMS** capability as shown in the following screenshot:

Select and configure capabilities

☑ Mapping (always enabled)	☐ WCS
☑ **WMS**	☐ Feature Access
☐ Schematics	☐ Mobile Data Access
☐ Network Analysis	☑ KML
☐ WFS	

WMS Configuration

URLs

URL: http://GIS-SERVER01:6080/arcgis/services/Parcels_from_sd/MapServer/WMSServer

Publishing the utility map service

In the coming exercises, we will be using some utility data along with some other data that I have provided with the book. We need to publish and register the geodatabase using the same techniques we learned in *Chapter 2, Authoring Web Services*. Download the book data from `www.packtpub.com`; you will find the utility data in `7364EN_03_Files\AGSA\Data\Utility.gdb`. Open the `Electricity.mxd` file in `7364EN_03_Files\AGSA\Documents`. I have already done the symbology and labeling work for you, so you don't need to worry about that part. Go ahead and publish the `Electricity` map service and make sure to enable the OGC WMS capability. This is just the start; we will publish more services as we progress through the chapter.

 When you open the `Electricity.mxd` file, the source might be lost; simply set the overhead power cable layer to the UNC path `\\GIS-SERVER01 \AGSA\Data\Utility.gdb\PowerCable` feature class. To do that, you must first share the folder `AGSA` as we did back in *Chapter 2, Authoring Web Services*. This is the best way you can successfully register the folder.

The following screenshot shows the utility data we just added to the map:

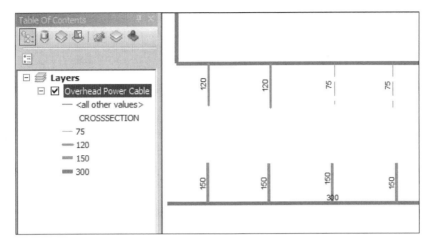

Using GIS services for visualization

The first thing that comes to mind when you want to use a map service is how you can see it, visualize it, present it, browse through it, and look for patterns—in other words, how you consume it. There are many tools that allow you to visualize the GIS services that you author in ArcGIS for Server, we will inspect and try out a few of them, and you can pick your favorite based on your preferences. We will also tackle how to consume your map services from well-known APIs such as JavaScript API. Don't worry! You do not need polished programming skills to do this; everything is made easy with a few lines of code, and you can compile and run a complete web page hosting your map services.

Consuming services from the GIS software

Since map services follow certain standards, they can be consumed from any software. We will explore the out-of-the-box software that has the capability to read map services.

Using ArcMap

ArcMap is a great tool to author and consume services. Esri has invested so many resources in developing and perfecting ArcMap that it has become a consolidated geography toolset. It is Esri's cash cow. Sometimes, I like to call ArcMap the "geosmith" of the GIS ecosystem, as most of the work we need to do can be done with this software. If you recall, in *Chapter 2, Authoring Web Services*, we consumed a map service from ArcMap to test our data. To avoid replicating information, you can refer to *Chapter 2, Authoring Web Services*, and rework the exercise in the *Testing the GIS services* section. Reading an OGC service from ArcMap is not difficult: to do that, we will need a WMS service (which we just published) enabled. Let us go and fetch the WMS service URL for the Electricity map service. To do that, we need to go to Manager, as we said before, and copy the WMS URL to the clipboard so you don't have to type the whole thing.

Open ArcMap and click on **Add Data** to add the utility WMS layer to the map. From **Catalog Tree**, select **GIS Servers** and then double-click on **Add WMS Server**. This will establish a connection with the WMS service. In the next form, paste or type in the WMS service URL for our Electricity service: http://GIS-SERVER01:6080/ arcgis/services/Electricity/MapServer/WMSServer. Again, it is recommended that you use a dedicated Web server if you have installed a Web Adaptor thus avoiding to point explicitly to the GIS servers. Click on **Get Layers** to establish the connection; if the connection is successful, you will be able to add the layer to the map. Click on **OK** and rename the connection to Electricity@GIS-SERVER01. You just created a WMS connection on the fly. We will now use this connection to read the WMS service. The screenshot of the WMS configuration is as follows:

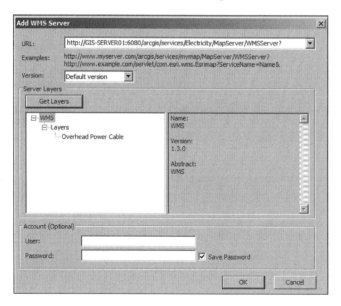

You can create the WMS connection from ArcCatalog as well.

Double-click on the `Electricity@GIS-SERVER01` connection you just created, select the `Electricity` service and click on **Add**. Refer the following screenshot:

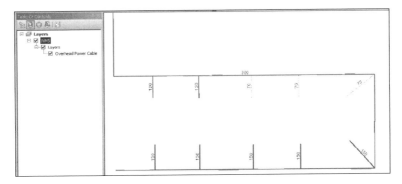

Now that we have added the utility layer as a WMS service, we can do basic zooming, panning, and even identifying. From the **Tools** toolbar, select the **Identify** tool and click on the red power cable to identify its attributes. You should get a small window with the basic attribute of that power cable. You can see that the voltage on the cable is 400 volts, and it is a large cable, around 300 mm^2 in diameter, and more than a kilometer in length. Refer the following table:

OBJECTID	SHAPE	VOLTAGE_V	CROSSSECTION_MM2	SHAPE_Length_M
1	Polyline	400	300	1441.9821

Using QGIS

We have managed to consume and browse the map services we authored in ArcMap; however, not everyone will have ArcMap to read this service. Plus, your map service is published in other formats, so it could be consumed by other software as well. There is plenty of GIS software out there, and many of these software are free, such as QGIS, GRASS, ArcGIS Explorer, gvSIG, and many others. My personal favorite is QGIS. We will be using this free software to browse our electric network on the WMS standard. QGIS is available on many platforms, including Windows, Linux, and Mac OS X. Recently, the team at QGIS compiled an Android version as well, so you can see how much time and resources have been spent on this product. QGIS supports WMS along with other OGC services. In this exercise, we learn how to use WMS service in QGIS and combine it with existing data. You can download QGIS Version 1.8 from www.qgis.org.

What you are about to do was an actual real scenario that I needed to resolve with one of my clients. Let us assume there are two departments, E and P, responsible for updating electric network and parcels respectively in separate geodatabases. Every time there is a new electric project, the department E checks for the latest parcels data in order to make the proper network design. Currently, E is getting parcels shape files on a yearly basis from the P department. So you can assume that the parcels might not be up to date. In this chapter data, you will find the file LandParcels2013.shp, which holds data for the land parcels in the year 2013. Let us assume you are an engineer at E and you are going to add the parcels shape file to QGIS to see if the new proposed electric project fits perfectly. Open QGIS, which you just installed, and on the toolbar, click on the **Add Vector Layer** button. From the **Add vector layer** form, select **File** and click on **Browse** to browse for LandParcels2013.shp in 7364EN_Chapter03_Files\AGSA\Data. Then, click on the **Open** button to add the data as shown in the following screenshot:

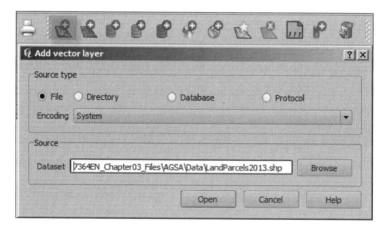

We need to do some work on this data, double-click on the LandParcels2013 layer, and the **Layer Properties** form will be displayed. In the **Style** tab, from the drop-down list which shows a single symbol, select **Categorized**. From the **Column** drop-down list, select **CATEGORY**, and finally, from the **Color ramp** drop-down list, select the blue color. Click on the **Classify** button and then on the **OK** button as shown in the following screenshot:

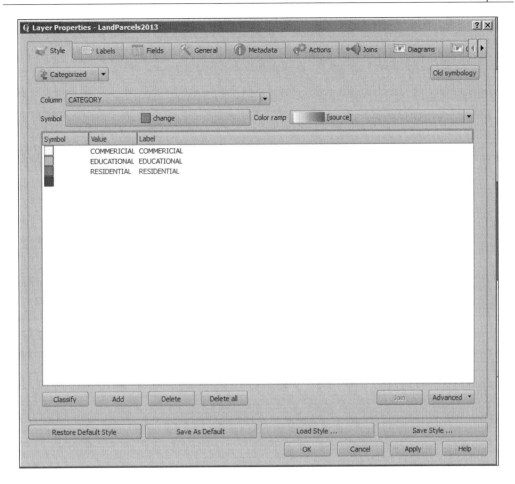

Once you do that, you will see that the symbology of the parcels changes to give each parcel a unique color, along with a legend, to describe it, as shown in the following screenshot:

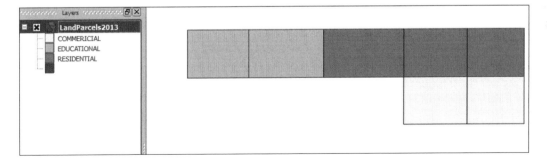

Now that we have the parcel data, we need to add our electric network to check it against the parcels to see if the wiring has been done properly or not. Fortunately, our latest data is already published as WMS, so let us add our electric network. From QGIS toolbar, click on the **Add WMS Layer** button; a form will be displayed. This form will have the list of all, WMS layers that you are going to add. In the **Add Layer(s) from a Server** form, click on **New** to add a new WMS layer, new form will pop up. In the **Name** field, type the name of the layer. Since we are adding an electricity layer, we will type `Electricity` in the **Name** field, and in the **URL** field, you can write your WMS URL that you got from ArcGIS for Server Manager in the beginning of this chapter. Leave the rest of the fields blank and click on the **OK** button, as shown in the following screenshot:

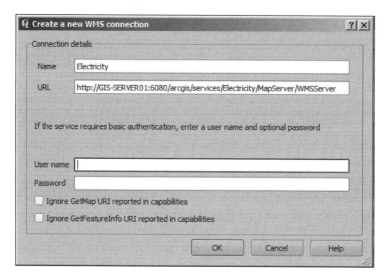

You will notice that the previous form will now have one layer in the drop-down list. Select **Electricity** from the drop-down list and then click on **Connect** to fetch the WMS layer information. From the tree view, select **0** as the layer ID (the **ID** column).

In the **Image Encoding** box, select **PNG** and then type `Power Cable` in the **Layer name** textbox. Finally, click on the **Add** button to add the layer to the QGIS map.

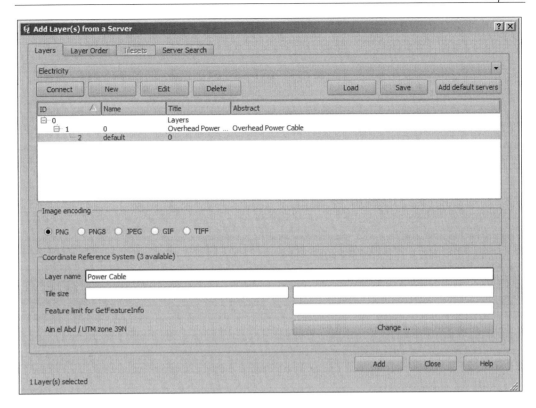

Now, you can see that the electricity layer has been added on top of the parcels, giving us a nice visual coloration to indicate which cable feeds which parcel. The following screenshot displays this representation:

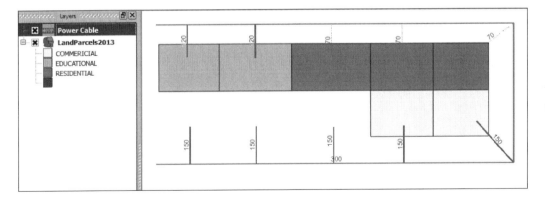

Best practice

WMS server offers many image encoding schemes; you have to use the format that suits your application. Choose JPEG and PNG encoding if you want fast loading, and choose TIFF if you want high resolution.

Clearly, you can see that the parcels data is not up-to-date, as there are three power cables with no parcels. This means your electric network is more up-to-date than the parcels, so we have to ask the P department to send us the new `Parcels` shape file. Alternatively, we could convince them to publish their `Parcels` service as WMS so that we can just use that instead of shape files. Fortunately, back in *Chapter 2, Authoring Web Services*, you did publish the `Parcels` service as WMS, so you may now use it. Now, we have a live WMS service pointing to the latest up-to-date `Parcels` database from the URL `http://GIS-SERVER01:6080/arcgis/ services/Parcels_FGDB/MapServer/WMSServer`. Let's add that to QGIS using the same approach and name it `Parcels`. Turn off the layer **LandParcels2013** and drag the **Power Cable** layer above `Parcels`. You will see that you got the full and up-to-date `Parcels` data, and it turns out that the three power cables were feeding three large commercial stores that happen to have been registered recently.

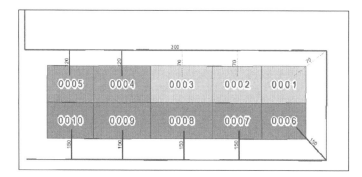

Using Google Earth

Google Earth is one of the clients that ArcGIS for Server supports. Some like to use Google Earth for its updated satellite imagery as a reference to overlay their data. With ArcGIS for Server, you can publish your services as KMZ files, which can be rendered by Google Earth. First, we will publish a new map service with the KML capability, using the skills you acquired in *Chapter 2, Authoring Web Services*. Let us open the map document I created for you. You can find it here: `7364EN_03_Files\ AGSA\Documents named US_States.mxd`. If the document loses its source data, simply point it back to the corresponding data in `7364EN_03_Files\AGSA\Data\ USS_states.gdb`. Share the document as a map service and make sure the KML is enabled. Leave everything to its default and name the map service `US_States`.

Now, we need to get the KML URL, which will allow Google Earth to fetch the data. The URL should look as follows:

```
http://<SERVER>/arcgis/rest/services/<SERVICE NAME>/MapServer/Kml/
mapImage.kmz
```

So our States service will be as follows:

```
http://GIS-SERVER01:6080/arcgis/rest/services/US_States/MapServer/
Kml/mapImage.kmz
```

We are almost ready; we now need to run Google Earth. Download Version 7.1 at `www.google.com/earth`, install the software, and run it. From the **Places** pane on the left-hand side, right-click on **My Places** and point to **Add** menu, then click on **Network Link**. On the **New Network Link** form, type `US States` in the **Name** field and the URL in **Link** field and click on the **OK** button:

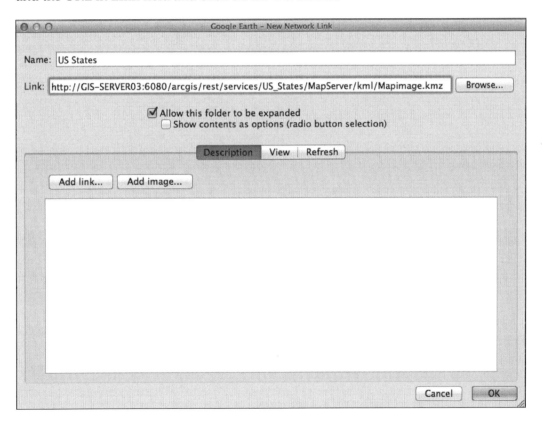

This will take a few moments until the KMZ file is downloaded and rendered by Google Earth. Once it is downloaded, you will start seeing it drawing on Google Earth.

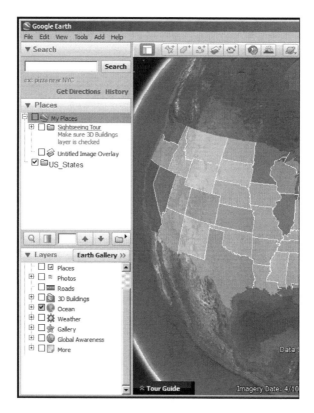

That looks good! You just added your map service on Google Earth. Think of all the applications that you could use this for. There is one more option we want to explore in Google Earth before we move on to the next section. Let us say you don't want to enable KML for security reasons, as you know KML files can be downloaded and shared offline. For that, you can either use KML network link or standardize your services and only permit the use of WMS service. Fortunately, Google Earth can consume OGC WMS services as well, so let us go back to the **US States** service in the ArcGIS Manager and enable the WMS capability. From the **My Places** section on the left-hand side under the **Places** pane, right-click on **My Places** and point to **Add**, then click on **Image Overlay**. In the pop-up form, type in US States WMS in the **Name** field and leave the **Link** field empty. Activate the **Refresh** tab and click on **WMS Parameters**. On the **Web Mapping Service Parameters** window, click on **Add** and then type in the **WMS URL**. Click on **OK** to commit the changes, and make sure the layer is under the selected layers. You will see the new WMS layer has been added on Google Earth.

Consuming services from APIs

We have published services and managed to find an out-of-the-box method to consume them without writing any lines of code, and that worked pretty well. However, there are times when you will need to write your own programs to consume your services. This is when you will use the APIs.

Winter is coming – the Flex and Silverlight APIs

There are several APIs that allow you to consume ArcGIS for Server services. Silverlight and Flex are two of the most used APIs that Esri invested in for years. Despite their ease of use and abundant resources, I will not be covering them in this book simply because they are not among the ascending technologies. They are also not supported on tablets and mobile devices and are alien to the new cloud technology, which is where everything is headed. They also require special plugins to run, while JavaScript runs natively on browsers. The debate between Silverlight and Flex versus JavaScript reminds me of how *Homo Neanderthal* and *Homo Heidelbergensis* went extinct because of us, *Homo Sapiens*. It might not be a fair comparison since the evolution of the latter spans millions of years as compared to these technologies; however, the three of these technologies spawned from the same web ecosystem, the *Homo Erectus*. Silverlight and Flex are technologies that have had their spring, and I believe it is more strategic for Esri to pour its time and resources into molding a full-fledged, rich JavaScript map viewer that developers can use and extend – the next ArcMap of the Web, the Web Geo Smith.

Using the ArcGIS JavaScript API

The ArcGIS JavaScript API uses a rich library built on top of **Dojo**, a JavaScript toolkit. This library allows clients to do so much more with maps. We will tackle two approaches to consume map services using the JavaScript API. The first one will be the online method; this is a simple method in which the JavaScript library is located on Esri servers, and it therefore requires an Internet connection to work. The second method is the offline method, where you will be able to download the library offline and run it without the need to connect to the Internet.

Online mode

Here, you will be able to use the JavaScript API. Make sure you have an Internet connection as we need to access the ArcGIS library necessary to render the map services that you are going to load. In this exercise, we will load the World data hosted by Esri on the REST URL `http://server.arcgisonline.com/ArcGIS/rest/services/World_Topo_Map/MapServer` into an HTML page using a few lines of JavaScript. The beauty of this is that all we need is a text editor, such as Notepad, and a web browser.

First, we will write the HTML file step by step, which will enable you to understand how the API works. Go ahead and open Notepad or your favorite text editor. I use Notepad++ since it is light, free, and supports many programming language syntaxes (you can download it from `www.notepad-plus-plus.org`). However, your Windows Notepad or Mac TextPad will do the same. Since we are writing an HTML file, we will start the basic HTML headers and skeleton as follows:

```
<html>

<header>

</header>

<body>

</body>

</html>
```

Save the file at `7364EN_03_Files\AGSA\Code` and name it `agsJS_Online_Mode.html`. Now, we will add our first HTML element in which the map will be drawn; it is a `div` element. Let us call it `MapCanvas`; we should add that in the `body` tag:

```
<html>

<header>

</header>

<body>
<div id ="MapCanvas">Here where the map should go</div>
</body>

</html>
```

Double-click on the HTML file to run it. Don't expect a map to pop up just yet. I just want to show you what you will get. You should get something like the following:

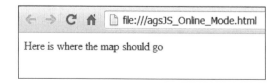

ArcGIS JavaScript API is on Version 3.6 now, but I'm going to use 3.5 as it is more stable.

Let us continue to add code to the HTML file, but first remove the text in MapCanvas, add the reference to the JavaScript library, and add the script tag to the header element, as shown in the following code:

```
<html>

<header>

<script src="http://js.arcgis.com/3.5/"></script>

</header>

<body>
<div id ="MapCanvas"> </div>
</body>

</html>
```

Still there is no map because this is just a reference; we need to use the functions in that library to create the map. Let us add another script tag; we will import the map library using the keyword dojo.require, and then we will add an empty function, startup. Using the keyword dojo.addonLoad, the script will call out startup function when the code is initialized successfully. To test this, we will add a small alert message in the startup function just to make sure things are working:

```
<html>
<header>
<script src="http://js.arcgis.com/3.5/"></script>

<script>

   dojo.require("esri.map");

Function startup()
{
  alert("map is about to initialize")

}

dojo.addOnLoad(startup);
```

```
</script>

</header>

<body>
<div id ="MapCanvas"> </div>
</body>
</html>
```

Open your HTML file, and you should see a small message box if JavaScript is enabled on your browser. The message box will look like the following screenshot:

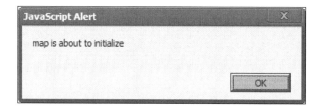

Remove the `alert` code, and let us add the code you are waiting for. We will now create a map object and then add a layer to that map. The line `map = new esri.Map()` takes our `div` element, `MapCanvas`, and creates a map object which will hold the layers that we add to it. To create a layer, we need to create a `ArcGISDynamicMapServiceLayer` object that will take our REST URL and then render it as a layer. The last line is `map.addlayer`, which will add the layer to the map. As shown in the following code, I have also added some style to our canvas to force the map to draw in fullscreen mode:

```
<html>
<header>
<script src="http://js.arcgis.com/3.5/"></script>

<script>

dojo.require("esri.map");

function startup()
{

  var map = new esri.Map("MapCanvas");

var layer = new esri.layers.ArcGISDynamicMapServiceLayer("http://
server.arcgisonline.com/ArcGIS/rest/services/World_Topo_Map/
MapServer");

  map.addLayer(layer);
```

```
}

dojo.addOnLoad(startup);

</script>
</header>
<body>

<div id ="MapCanvas" style = "height: 100%;width:100%" > </div>

</body>
</html>
```

Run your code and you will finally see your map. You can add necessary effects to make your page look good. There are plenty of JavaScript API examples that can be found at resources.esri.com. You will see the following map after running the code:

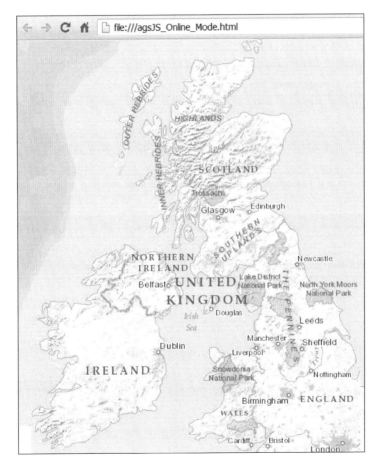

You can use the same piece of code to load your local services; let us load our `Parcels` and `Electricity` REST map services. It is recommended that you use a dedicated Web server; however, it is ok to use the built-in Web server to get the URL. Either will work; refer to *Chapter 2, Authoring Web Services*, to learn the differences between the two.

> **Best practice**
>
> Remember it is recommended that you use a dedicated Web server when you expose your services so that you can utilize the power of your GIS servers.

This following code will allow you to view both services:

```
<html>
<header>
<script src="http://js.arcgis.com/3.5/"></script>
<script>

dojo.require("esri.map");

function startup()
{
var map = new esri.Map("MapCanvas");

var parcelsLayer = new esri.layers.ArcGISDynamicMapServiceLayer(
"http://WEB-SERVER01/wa/rest/services/Parcels/MapServer"
);

var electriclayer = new esri.layers.ArcGISDynamicMapServiceLayer(
"http://WEB-SERVER01/wa/rest/services/Electricity/MapServer"
);

map.addLayer(parcelsLayer);
map.addLayer(electriclayer);

}
dojo.addOnLoad(startup);
</script>
</header>
<body>
<div id ="MapCanvas" style = "height: 100%;width:100%" > </div>

</body>
</html>
```

And the output of this code will be as follows:

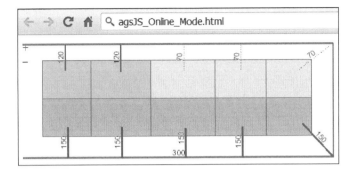

Offline mode

Most organizations don't allow Internet access on their servers for security reasons, they run everything off the intranet. In this case, the online mode for JavaScript API development will not be of use. There is a way to download the ArcGIS JavaScript API library and reference it on your websites; we will learn how to do that in this section. Before you start, make sure you install IIS—if you haven't done that already. You can use your Web server, `WEB-SERVER01`, which you can find at the `7364EN_03_Files\AGSA\jsapi35` folder. Copy the folder `arcgis_js_api` to `c:\inetpub\wwwroot` and then open your text editor and write the same code you used in online mode. We will make a slight change to the reference: we will point to the library we just copied to `WEB-SERVER01`.

You can replace `WEB-SERVER01` with `GIS-SERVER01` if you are using the express installation; just make sure that IIS is installed and that the path `c:\inetpub\` is valid.

```
<html>
<header>
<script src="http://WEB-SERVER01/arcgis_js_api/library/3.5/3.5/init.
js"></script>
<script>

dojo.require("esri.map");

function startup()
{
var map = new esri.Map("MapCanvas");

var parcelsLayer = new esri.layers.ArcGISDynamicMapServiceLayer(
"http://WEB-SERVER01/wa/rest/services/Parcels/MapServer"
);
```

```
var electriclayer = new esri.layers.ArcGISDynamicMapServiceLayer(
"http://WEB-SERVER01/wa/rest/services/Electricity/MapServer"
);

map.addLayer(parcelsLayer);
map.addLayer(electriclayer);

}
dojo.addOnLoad(startup);
</script>
</header>
<body>
<div id ="MapCanvas" style = "height: 100%;width:100%" > </div>

</body>
</html>
```

Save the file to `c:\inetpub\wwwroot` and name it `agsJS_Offline_Mode.html`. To run the page, open Chrome, type the following, and hit *Enter*:

`http://WEB-SERVER01/agsJS_Offline_Mode.html`

You can now access this URL from any machine in the same network to browse your map services. If you are connected to Wi-Fi, you can even browse it from your mobile or tablet. I have provided you with the two files `agsJS_Online_Mode_Original.html` and `agsJS_Offline_Mode_Original.html`. You can find them at `7364EN_03_Files\AGSA\Code`. They have slightly more code to adjust the layout, and they use a bit of **Cascade Style Sheets (CSS)**, styles used in HTML documents.

Using GIS services for editing

Editing GIS services is challenging. It requires some steps, and unfortunately, there is no single well-documented and consolidated resource that discusses this section. Therefore, I made this section as detailed as possible. Editing data through a GIS service is useful in many scenarios. I can think of a scenario where this might prove to be of use; let us take the case of incident reporting. If you find something in the road—a blown main pipe or a sparking power cable—you would want to report it immediately as you really don't have the time to drive to the office and connect to your geodatabase where your data is stored and start editing incidents then. It would be much more efficient if you were able to directly access your geodatabase from your laptop, or smart phone while you are on the site, add the incident, and sync it with the geodatabase. A GIS service that can be edited is called a feature service. In this section, we will create a new feature class on an enterprise geodatabase, publish a feature service, and then edit it in ArcMap.

Prerequisites

There are a number of things you need before you can edit a feature service. First of all, you should know that you cannot edit a feature service that is pointing to a personal geodatabase; your database should be an enterprise SDE geodatabase. I have an SQL Server enterprise geodatabase; you may also use PostgreSQL, which can be downloaded for free at www.postgresql.org. Next, it is recommended that you use database authentication instead of operating system authentication or else you will run into problems. Database authentication can be controlled, whereas operating system authentication, while effective, requires all GIS servers to have operating system authentication access to the database. This might not always be the case and you will run into problems while registering the data store. Lastly, your geodatabase should be registered in the ArcGIS for Server data store, and your data should be registered as versioned in the SDE, with options to move edits to the base. We will now perform all these steps.

Setting up the SDE geodatabase

First, we need to create the database user that will be able to connect to and edit the geodatabase. If you already have an SDE geodatabase ready, you may skip this step. Log in to your enterprise geodatabase server — mine is SDE-SERVER01 — and open **SQL Server Management Studio**, connect using the sa user or any user that have database administrator privileges. The sa user is created by default when you install the SQL Server. From the **Object Explorer** tree view, expand the Security folder and then right-click on **Logins** and select **New Login**; this will pop up a new window. In the **Login name** field, type agsEditor and select **SQL Server authentication**. Type the password in the **Password** and **Confirm password** fields, and make sure to uncheck the **Enforce password policy** if you are not worried about sophisticated passwords right now. From the **Default database** drop-down list, select your geodatabase, which should be SDE. On the **Select a page** list, click on **User Mapping** to set the permissions and select the SDE database to map it. From the **Database role membership** window for SDE, check db_datareader and db_datawriter so you give read and write access to the user agsEditor. Lastly, we will perform one more temporary step; we will assign agsEditor to the sysadmin server role so the user can manage the geodatabase. Click on **Server Roles** and check the **sysadmin** role and click on **OK** to save.

 The sysadmin server role is assigned so the agsEditor user can also create a feature class; you will need it in this exercise. However, if your feature classes are already created, you may revoke it safely.

Connecting and registering the SDE geodatabase

If you already have an enterprise geodatabase set up, make sure you have the agsEditor user with read/write privileges and you will be ready. Go to your publisher machine, GIS-SERVER01, or the machine that has an ArcGIS for Desktop installation so that we can connect to the geodatabase. Make sure you have your 64-bit DBMS client installed on this machine and every other GIS server, as discussed in the previous chapters. Open ArcCatalog; from the **Catalog Tree** menu, expand the **Database Connections** option and double-click on **Add Database Connection** to create a new connection. In the **Database Connection** window, select **SQL Server** from the **Database Platform** drop-down list and type in the **Instance** field the geodatabase server name — SDE-SERVER01 — of your SDE server. You can use the IP Address here as well. In the **Authentication Type** drop-down menu, select **Database Authentication** and type in the database credentials of the user profile we have just created. Then, select **SDE** from the **Database** drop-down list so we connect to this database. In case you have multiple geodatabases on your server, click on **OK** and rename the connection to agsEditor@SDEServer.

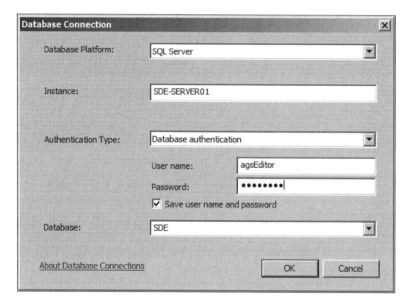

 If you are using a database other than SQL Server, select it from the **Database Platform** dropdown.

Now, it is time to register the geodatabase in the data store, we did this exercise back in section *Registering with an enterprise geodatabase* in *Chapter 2, Authoring Web Services*. Use the `agsEditor@SDEServer` SDE file to register this connection in the Server data store. Now, we need to create the feature class that we will edit; this is the `Incidents` feature class. It is a point feature class that we will use to log incidents in our geodatabase. The feature class is already created for you, so you can simply copy and paste it in your geodatabase. From ArcCatalog, connect to the book data folder `7364EN_03_Files\AGSA\Data`, double-click on the `Incidents` file geodatabase, and then right-click on the `Incidents` feature class and click on **Copy**. Go to `agsEditor@SDEServer` and double-click on the connection to open it; right-click on it and paste the feature class there. Now, we need to enable versioning on our feature class so we can edit it; to do that, right-click on the `Incidents` feature class, select **Manage** and then click on **Register As Versioned**. This will enable editing on this feature class. A new window will pop up, and you should check the option **Register the selected objects with the option to move edits to base** and then click on **OK**. This option is necessary so that any edits are moved directly to the base tables instead of waiting for an SDE compress operation to do it.

Publishing a feature service

We took some time to set up the enterprise geodatabase. We are now ready to publish our feature service, and we need to Geo Smith for that. Open ArcMap and click on **Add Data** to add the `Incidents` feature class by connecting to `agsEditor@SDEServer`. We will now create a feature template. These are templates introduced in ArcGIS 10 and allow the editor to save a template of a feature with values and symbology and use it to simplify the editing process. The feature template will be used later to edit the feature service. From ArcMap, activate the **Editor** toolbar and click on **Start Editing**. From the **Create Feature dockable** window, double-click on the `Incidents` template; this is the default template created, and we will change it. Name the template `Power Surge` and change the symbology to match the next figure.

To do

From the **Manage Templates** window, create another template for water leaks.

Now that we have a template ready for editing, let us publish this map. Give it the name `Incidents_FS` and make sure you have registered the geodatabase in the Server site data store before you continue, or you will run into problems. In the **Service Editor** window, click on **Capabilities** and check the **Feature Access** option. Click on **Publish** and this will publish our service as a feature service. You can imagine that a feature service will have a unique URL as well, which differs from the map service URL.

Alternatively, you can use the `Incidents.mxd` file, which I already created with the symbology and feature templates. However, you have to set the data source to your local enterprise geodatabase service.

Editing feature services using ArcMap

We have successfully published the feature service. Now it is time to put it to use and start editing it. Open ArcMap and click on **Add Data**. Connect to your Server site and add the `Incidents_FS` feature service. You will notice two instances of `Incidents_FS`: one will be a **Map Service** type, and the second one will be a **Feature Service** type. Make sure to select the **Feature Service** type and also make sure to add the `Parcels` and `Electricity` map services.

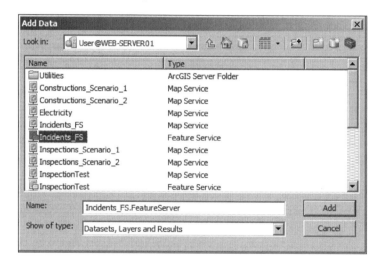

Unfortunately, while working with feature services, you can't just start editing from the editor toolbar and start working. To edit a feature service, ArcGIS for Server should copy a portion of the data in the current extent locally. We can start working normally on this local data after our work is finished and saved. We run a process called synchronization to synchronize our edits with those in the feature service. Now that this is explained, let us start. In the **Table of Content** window in ArcMap, right-click on the `Incidents_FS` group layer—which holds the feature service—and point to **Edit Features**. Then, click on **Create Local Copy for Editing**, as shown in the following screenshot. This will create a file geodatabase locally for you to edit.

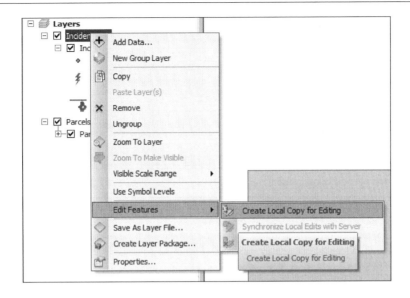

Now that the source of your Incidents_FS group layer is now set to a local file geodatabase, point to the editor toolbar and click on **Start Editing**. Add a **Power Surge** feature on the power cable and add a **Water Leak** feature near any house. From the editing toolbar, click on **Save Editing** and then on **Stop Editing**. To synchronize the edits back with the feature service, right click on the Incidents_FS group layer, point to **Edit Features**, and then click on **Synchronize Local Edits with Server**.

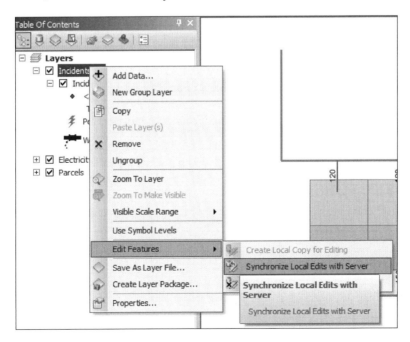

You have just created a feature service and edited it successfully in ArcMap. To test it further, get a laptop and install ArcGIS for Desktop on it. Connect it to the LAN, and try editing the feature service from there. You will notice that you do not need to have the geodatabase clients installed on the machine you are editing, which makes this a portable solution. If you do not have access to the Server site, you still can edit your data with the option **Disconnect local copy from Server**. With this, you can take your laptop to the field, edit there, and then return to the office to reconnect to Server and sync your edits.

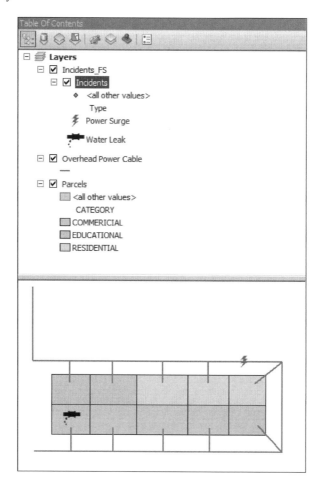

Using GIS services for analysis

We have learned how to visualize our services, overlay more than one service together, and even write code to consume the services. Now, we need to put these services to use. We will do this by asking a question and trying to answer it by analyzing the different map services and trying to use the power of GIS. Put on your detective hat and let us start!

Prerequisites

Before we start, we need to publish some more new map services, Inspection, Construction, and Outage for each scenario. You can find their map documents at Chapter03\Code\7364EN_03_Files\AGSA\Documents. The Inspections_Scenario1, Inspections_Scenario2, Outage_Scenario1, and Outage_Scenario2 files can be located in the Utility geodatabase, while Constructions_Scenario1 and Constructions_Scenario2 are polygon feature classes that can be found in the Projects geodatabase.

To do

Publish the map documents Constructions_Scenario_1.mxd, Constructions_Scenario_2.mxd, Inspections_Scenario_1.mxd, Inspections_Scenario_2.mxd, Outage_Scenario_1.mxd, and Outage_Scenario_2.mxd as map services with default settings. If the source of the data is lost, set it to the UNC path of the corresponding geodatabase.

We will now use these services in our analysis. You can use ArcMap or Quantum GIS for analysis; I will be using ArcMap.

Finding the outage cause – scenario 1

You have been assigned the task analyzing the call logs of customers with electricity outages and trying to find the cause of the outages. When a customer reports an outage, the **Outage Management System (OMS)** will automatically record their call and update the outage database with the timestamp. The outages are already available as a real-time map service, which you can use to analyze the outages. In this scenario, there have been three outages on the electric network on the same area and you are asked to find the cause. The inspections and projects departments have given you access to their live data to help you with the analysis.

First, we need to create a user connection to our Server site, which hosts all the map services we need. This connection will provide us with a read-only view of our services. You may refer to the *Testing the GIS Services* section of *Chapter 2, Authoring Web Services*, which explains how to accomplish this. Open ArcMap and click on **Add Data** to add our services. Then, open your Server site connection and add these map services to your map to start the analysis: Electric, Parcels, and Outage_Scenario_1. On the **Tools** toolbar, click on **Full Extent** to zoom to the full extent of the data. Then, drag the layers in the order **Outages**, **Electricity**, and **Parcels** to the bottom so the layers will be drawn in the correct order. Your map should look like the following screenshot:

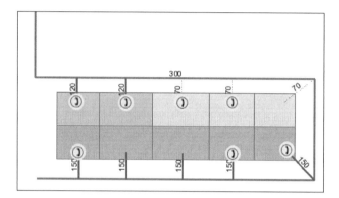

Note that there are a number of outages spread along the power cable and remember that all of them may not be represented here. There may be other outages that were not reported simply because the owner is not at home. We have to work with what we have and try to find the fault. From the magnitude of the outages, they all seem related to a single cause. If it is a single outage, we can narrow it down to the house itself. Therefore, we need more data to help us in our analysis. We will start by checking whether there are any other projects in the area that might have caused this. Go ahead and add the Constructions_Scenario_1 map service, which you can get by connecting to the projects department Server site (in this case, it is basically the same Server site).

There are two construction projects in the area. As you can see, they are far from our electric network (as shown in the following screenshot), so it is unlikely that they are the cause of the problem.

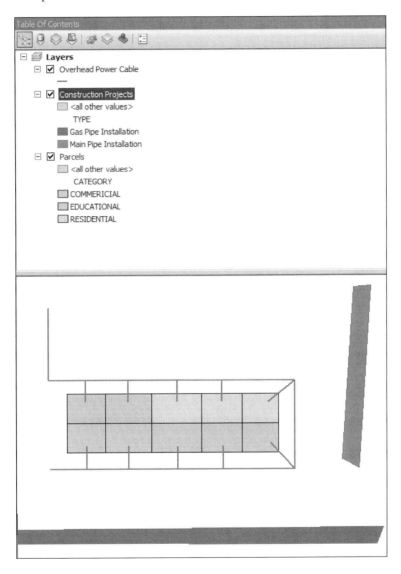

Since there are no projects in the area, let us see if there were any recent inspections; for that, we call the inspections department to provide us with a map service of their latest inspections. Fortunately, we have this. Let us add it, connect to the inspection department Server site and add the `Inspections` map service to the map, as shown in the following screenshot. From what we can see, there is one inspection in progress. If you use the **Identify** tool to check the type of inspection, you will find that it is a routine substation maintenance, which is most probably the cause of all the outages in this area.

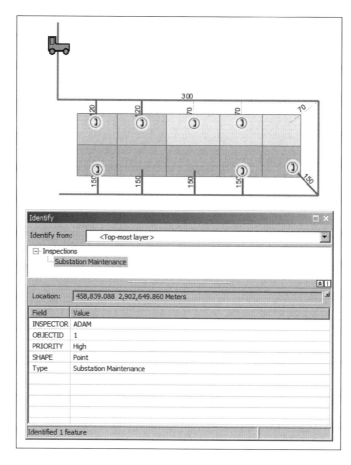

Problem solved! Let us dispatch a message to all customers to inform them that there is maintenance work going on in their area and it should wind up within the next hour. Here you can see how we quickly used multiple map services to analyze and solve a real-life problem. Let us move to the second scenario.

Finding the outage cause – scenario 2

In the first scenario, we managed to identify the reason behind the outages swiftly with the use of map services. Open ArcMap and click on **Add Data** to add our services. Open your Server site connection and add these map services to your maps to start the analysis: `Electric`, `Parcels`, and `Outage_Scenario_2`. From the **Tools** toolbar, click on **Full Extent** to zoom to the full extent of the data. Then, drag the layers in order **Outages**, **Electricity**, and **Parcels** to the bottom so the layers will be drawn in the correct order. According to the OMS outage log, it is clear that five adjacent commercial locations have been hit with an unknown, major outage, The rest of the houses seem to be running normally. You are asked to find out what caused the outage. The following screenshot illustrates the outage:

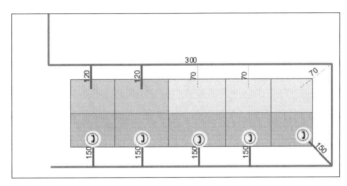

Since an inspection caused the previous scenario, let us check whether this scenario is also due to an inspection. Connect to the inspections Server site and add the `Inspections_Scenario_2` map service and take a close look at the result:

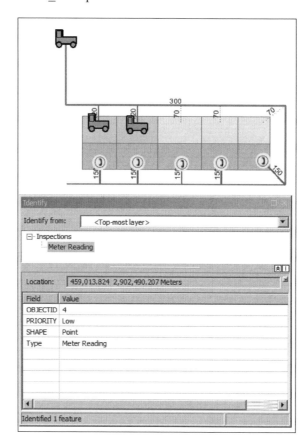

It looks like there are some inspections in the area. If you use the **Identify** tool, you will see that they are low-priority meter readings and are on the other side of the outage: they couldn't possibly have caused this outage. There must be something else that caused it. Since we have access to the projects data, we can add the `Constructions_Scenario_2` map service to add the construction data; let us resume our analysis.

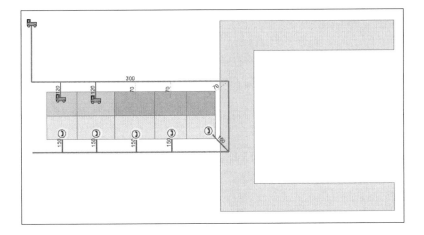

This must be the cause as there is a huge main pipe installation construction project running on the right-hand side of our electric network. This excavation may have caused one of the overhead power cable poles to fall, thus damaging the power cable and affecting all the customers fed downstream.

Meanwhile, on the GIS servers

There is a lot going on while we were consuming these services; let us take a moment to explore that. All the work we have been doing—whether it was visualizing, editing, or analyzing—is being done on the GIS servers. The GIS servers eventually receive the REST or SOAP request and process it. For instance, we always used a URL to connect to the Server site in the visualization section. The Server site then determines, based on history, which GIS server from the list of machines registered to the site is available and forwards the request to it. The GIS server then processes the request: if the request was to zoom in to a particular parcel, the GIS server queries the geodatabase, fetches the data within that extent, and then draws the map based on the selected protocol or standard. Whether to return it as a PNG image, KML, or SOAP XML is all based on the specified protocol. It is important to note that when a user is trying to connect to a map service using a hard REST URL, such as `http://GIS-SERVER01:6080/arcgis/`, which points directly to one of the GIS servers. The `GIS-SERVER01` is playing two roles here: that of a Web server that connects to the Server site and fetches the site configuration, and that of a GIS server to crunch the request. Therefore, if `GIS-SERVER01` is down, busy, or unreachable for any reason, the user has to wait although the Server site might have other GIS servers free. That is why I keep reminding you to use a dedicated Web server—something like `http://WEB-SERVER01/arcgis/`—so that the request is properly load balanced. We will have plenty to discuss about that in *Chapter 6, Clustering and Load Balancing*.

Summary

This chapter was full of practical exercises. You have done a lot of work with Server by now and know how powerful this product is. You now know how to consume the services you created in *Chapter 2, Authoring Web Services*, for visualization, editing, and analysis. You have used different GIS clients to consume these services and you have even written your own code to achieve that. You can see how diverse ArcGIS for Server is. You have data lying on your database, and Server allowed you to expose your GIS data to services supporting multiple standards and protocols. This made them capable of being used conveniently from multiple end points.

In the next chapter, we will discuss how to plan and design GIS services by analyzing their requirements.

4
Planning and Designing GIS Services

If you are in a production environment, there are factors that should be considered before publishing GIS services. While your entire library of data could be published as GIS services, it does not mean that you should do this. Publishing services is an expensive process, it tends to consume a lot of resources and server power and has to be maintained regularly. Therefore, it is recommended that you plan the services you are going to author. This chapter will cover two main topics: **planning** and **designing**.

The planning stage consists of two steps: The first step is acquiring and analyzing the requirements. This answers questions such as what is it that you want to accomplish? Why do you chose to publish services as your solution? Can your problem be solved more efficiently with a direct connection to the geodatabase? The second step involves the decision of what parts of your geodatabase should be exposed as GIS services. This should be based on the analysis carried out in the first step.

In the designing stage, you will learn how to design services you select and explicitly revise more concrete details in the process. You will answer questions such as what standards will the GIS services support? Which clients will consume your services? Will you publish each layer as a service, or multiple layers in a service? Each has its pros and cons and we will discuss these in this chapter. I believe it is better to kick-start this chapter with a case study. This way, you will be able to link the planning stage to your problem and act accordingly.

Case study of Bestaurants – the restaurants locator in Belize

Belize is thriving in tourism. Lots of tourists go there on holiday to enjoy its beautiful beaches and wide range of restaurants. The Government of Belize is trying to enrich tourists' experience in finding their favorite restaurants in the country more effectively. To accomplish that, a new project titled **Bestaurants** has been proposed, with which tourists can find restaurants on their mobile phone or through kiosks that the government will provide at different locations in the country. The Belize government keeps records of all its landmarks, including beaches, entertainment venues, bars, restaurants, cafes, saloons, and so on, in an Excel document that is updated regularly, along with a collection of images and promotional videos of the landmarks available for free to the tourists. You are required to design a solution using ArcGIS for Server that will allow tourists to find restaurants near their locations and filter them by category and rating. The solution should also provide an option of finding the most popular restaurants in Belize. You can find the Excel sheet in the chapter files package `7364EN_04_Files\AGSA\Data`, which can be downloaded from `www.packtpub.com`.

Planning GIS services

From what you have read in the case study, you may have realized that the solution cannot be implemented directly. There is some infrastructure that needs to be built. There is no database and there are no explicit networking requirements, so we have some freedom when it comes to planning. Therefore, we can start analyzing the requirements and come up with an optimal solution, which is the sole purpose of the planning stage. You are instructed to specifically use a server, which means that the Belize government might have already done its research and selected the server as its underlining infrastructure for this and future implementations.

Analyzing requirements

Let's start with the main goal of this study. Our solution needs to visualize the restaurants in the country, so I'm thinking there must be a map—a **basemap**—that contains basic geographic land cover of the country. There is no mention of such data in the case study. This map requires the restaurants' data source, hence we must have these records in a database, which is not the case here either. We only have an Excel document of all Belize landmarks that happens to include the restaurants. We need to find a way to filter this information out of the file. To visualize the restaurants on the map, the map requires the coordinates of each place.

We also need tourists to differentiate between restaurants, cafes, and bars. There must be some sort of categorization that we can later create symbology for. Finally, it is required that tourists can find restaurants located near them and can find the most popular restaurants. Therefore, we should enable the query capability on this data so that users can search based on the current GPS location or by specifying an explicit query. Finally, there is a media repository for these restaurants that we should link and take into consideration while designing our database.

Nominating GIS services

Now, we will decide what GIS services we might need to plan based on the requirements that we have analyzed before. To give you a better idea of the planning process, I propose two options, and will assess the feasibility of each in the design phase. This means we will need to come up with two designs later and implement them accordingly.

Option 1 – single service

The first option is to propose a single GIS service that will hold all of this information. Regardless of how we will design this service, we should be able to visualize restaurants, cafes, and bars in Belize, and differentiate between them with proper symbology based on the category. Users can also query this service to find restaurants based on a location or a particular filter.

Option 2 – multiple services

The second option is to plan multiple services instead of a single one. Why you would do this, however, is something that I will answer in the design stage, in which you will choose your preferences. In this case, we propose three GIS services: Restaurants, Cafes, and Bars, each isolated in a separate service. All three services should be included along with the base map in the platform that will be used.

Designing GIS services

Now that we have planned which services should be authored, we need to create the blueprint of the services and their design. Also, we have to decide what the underlying database design is, how the services will be authored, and what standards they will support. We will get to these technical questions in the coming pages. Note that we proposed two options in the planning stage, so we need to produce two designs. I usually use the **Unified Modelling Language (UML)** as a tool for designing GIS services, specifically the deployment diagram as it provides a good blueprint of the GIS services design. There are plenty of UML books out there if you want to get into it: my favorite is *UML Distilled* by *Martin Fowler*. As for the database design, we will use the entity-relationship diagram.

Database design

There is no database mentioned in the case study, and no database means no geodatabase. This means we cannot create GIS services without a geodatabase. So, we need to come up with a design for this database. This design should cater to the requirements analyzed in the planning stage. A weak design could cause your solution to collapse, and could be very expensive to repair. Let's take a look at the Belize landmarks Excel sheet provided with the case study. Go ahead and open the `Belize_Landmarks.xls` file in files package `7364EN_04_Files\AGSA\Data`. I have copied a few records here. Take a look, and you will find there are some useful fields: **Category** and **SubCategory**, **Longitude** and **Latitude** information (which is very important to georeference the restaurants), and finally, the **Rating** of a landmark.

ID	Name	Category	SubCategory	Longitude	Latitude	Rating
1	Raggamuffin Tours	Activities	Activities	-88.02370166	17.74716893	7
3	Habaneros	Food and Drink	Restaurants	-88.0243206	17.74274661	10
4	Amor Y Café	Food and Drink	Cafes	-88.02455832	17.74232287	8
5	I&I Reggae Bar	Food and Drink	Bars	-88.02535194	17.74058384	7
6	Bamboo Grill	Food and Drink	Restaurants	-88.02352708	17.74389439	10
7	The Split	Sights	Sights	-88.02352708	17.74389439	4

 You can convert this Excel sheet into a shape file and use it to publish the map service. However, a proper geodatabase is recommended, such as a personal, file, or enterprise.

The Entity-relationship diagram

There are many tools to create the **entity-relationship (ER)** diagram. Microsoft Visio is one of them, however, since I'm between Mac and Windows I like to use **Gliffy**. This is an HTML5 online sketching tool that is very useful for creating various design diagrams including UML and ER. You can save up to five diagrams with the free version and export it into various formats. You can access Gliffy from www.gliffy.com.

 Entity Relationship (ER, sometimes ERD or ERM) is a data model for describing the elements and relations between the database elements.

If you look into the requirements, you will find that there are three main categories: **Restaurants**, **Cafes**, and **Bars**. So, one might think that we can create three tables. While denormalizing tables can be good for optimization, it is a high-maintenance and inefficient design for three main reasons that I can think of. First, new categories might be introduced later, thus a new table needs to be created for each category. The second reason is that some information might be repeated among the three tables. Another reason is for any future maintenance, for example, joins and indexing you would carry out on all these tables is not very efficient.

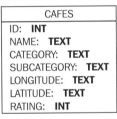

RESTAURANTS		BARS		CAFES	
ID:	**INT**	ID:	**INT**	ID:	**INT**
NAME:	**TEXT**	NAME:	**TEXT**	NAME:	**TEXT**
CATEGORY:	**TEXT**	CATEGORY:	**TEXT**	CATEGORY:	**TEXT**
SUBCATEGORY:	**TEXT**	SUBCATEGORY:	**TEXT**	SUBCATEGORY:	**TEXT**
LONGITUDE:	**TEXT**	LONGITUDE:	**TEXT**	LONGITUDE:	**TEXT**
LATITUDE:	**TEXT**	LATITUDE:	**TEXT**	LATITUDE:	**TEXT**
RATING:	**INT**	RATING:	**INT**	RATING:	**INT**

We will stick with one table containing all the categories and will import whatever fields the Excel document has into this table The second thing is that there are pictures and videos linked to each landmark, so we can consider adding two new **Binary Large Object (BLOB)** columns to our table.

 BLOB is an array of binary data stored in a single database field. Any file type can fit into a BLOB field.

The BLOB data type is good for storing raw pictures and video formats. In this case, we use one for the picture of the landmark and one for the video promotion.

There is a limitation to this design. There might be multiple pictures for the same landmark, however, this design permits one picture and one video for each landmark. I don't think Belize tourists will be so thrilled with this, so we need to fix it. To solve this limitation, we can add a new table that will hold the media of all landmarks and then add a one-to-many relationship between these two tables. This way, a landmark can have multiple pictures and videos. We can also add two more text columns for a picture and video description.

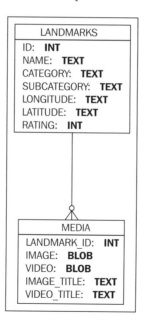

This looks much better. I think this will be enough to satisfy the study requirements. However, I am skeptical about whether the database could hold all these large media files, and it could eventually slow the performance of our queries. Moreover, what happens when you want to assign a new video or a picture to a landmark? There must be a custom interface. What about editing an existing picture? Can the administrator retrieve and change a BLOB field? Although the design is correct, it is not an efficient one. To fix this, we can move all pictures and videos into a dedicated Web server separated from the database; we basically link the images and videos there. What is even better is that we could upload the videos to YouTube and provide the URL, thus saving lots of space. Plus, tourists can share the YouTube link with their friends, which means more exposure for Belize! So, we can now change the BLOB fields into texts.

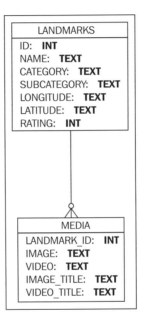

We just relieved the database with our design; this should be our final ERD. Let's add the final touches, the primary and foreign keys.

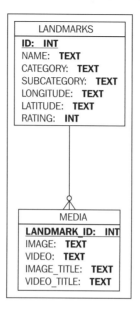

Optimizing using the database indexing

Indexing is a database technique that helps optimizing queries carried out frequently in a particular column. It basically analyzes the column data and organizes it in a way so that the search can be done much more efficiently. From the planning stage, we learned that users of the system will need to query the GIS service to find restaurants nearby. Therefore, it is good to enable indexing on the columns that will be used. Note that not all of the categories in the database will be visualized. For instance, it is not required for us to show activities, so we need to filter those out as we can't delete these records; the latter would mean tampering with the database. We can't hide them either, so we need a query to display only those landmarks that fall under the Food and Drink category. The **Structured Query Language (SQL)** query will be something like the following:

```
SELECT * FROM LANDMARKS WHERE CATEGORY = 'Food and Drink';
```

Unfortunately, we cannot model indexes in the ER diagram, but we can implement it using our favorite DBMS.

 SQL is a special programming language designed for data retrieval and manipulation on a relational database.

GIS services design

Designing GIS services is an essential process when you are building an infrastructure for an organization. You have to properly study your requirements, like we did in the previous section, and propose the goals from these requirements. Then you can stir your solution toward that goal using the design techniques. Therefore, any service we propose should be necessary and should serve that goal. It should be designed to fit the requirements. We have proposed two options in the planning stage, so we need to make two UML designs.

Option 1 – single map service

As the name suggests, the single service design consists of one service that holds all the restaurants. The way we model this, however, is entirely up to us. A service is basically a map document published on Server and contains layers pointing to the database. Now that we have designed the database, we need to apply the design for the GIS service data. I could start with a very simple design, the **Food and Drink** layer. This layer includes the three categories: Restaurants, Bars, and Cafes. Since the Landmarks table contains all landmarks, we create a definition query in the layer to filter out only those objects that belong to the Food and Drink category. In a deployment diagram, we usually model the servers and their components and how they are communicating. In this case, we have two servers. First, the database server with one database instance, `BelizeDB`, that has our database design implemented.

Second is a server to hold ArcGIS for Server, in which we should include our food and drink service. In that service, there is one layer that points to the database server, specifically the landmarks table.

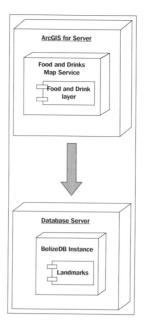

Let's think about this. If we went ahead and published that service, what would our tourists see? They will see all food and drinks in a layer. They don't actually know what a layer is, but I suppose we can make a little legend on the side to tell them what is what.

Let's assume that it is a tourist's bachelor party and he is planning to drop by all the bars in Belize tonight. He uses this system to locate nearby bars, but what he sees is simply everything. He asked if he could hide the Restaurants and Cafes and show only the bars. Guess what? You can't help! Anyone familiar with GIS will know that you cannot just turn off a symbology, you can either turn off an entire layer or nothing. So, we found a little problem with our design. To fix that, we need to separate each category in a layer.

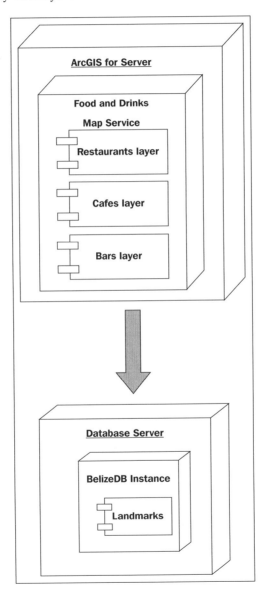

Option 2 – multiple map services

The other option is to publish the layers we authored as separate services. In other words, the Restaurants, Bars, and Cafes each go into a separate dedicated service. We will get to know why we would want to do that in this section. There are many incidents where you want your services detached from one another: better resource management, tightened security, or sometimes even optimization. The UML deployment diagram of a multiservice version of our solution looks like the following:

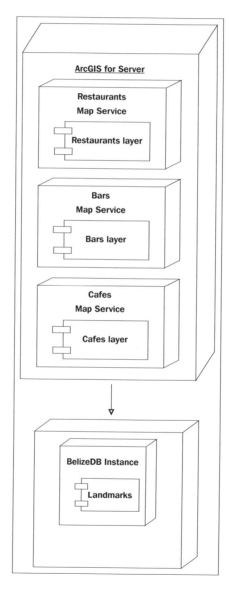

Single or multiple service designs

Comparing the two options really depends on the requirements. The two proposed designs will hold up in the implementation stage. You can run further analysis to test the robustness of your designs and finally select one. There are pros and cons to each option here. If you took the first option, a single service design is a good solution, particularly if you want to consume less resources. One service will hold all your data, thus ensuring data integrity. You can easily update your data and republish the service conveniently. Moreover, if something went wrong with your data, you have a single point of management, instead of managing multiple services. However, the downside with single service design is that you will have limited security control, because ArcGIS for Server maintain logs on the services level rather than the data level. So, whatever design you pick eventually should be made based on a trade-off. If you don't care much about security and control, you can slam all your data into a single service. However, if you have large data and you need to set privileges on who can access what, a multiservice design will probably work better for you.

Deploying GIS services

In the deployment stage, we go from abstract design, where we have everything, such as documents, diagrams, and flow charts, to concrete implementation, where we need to explicitly select what systems we need to interact with. The selection depends on what DBMS will manage our database and the other steps required for the implementation. I mentioned a very important stage that I cannot model in the design, which is how to convert our database into a geodatabase and then use it to publish our services.

Enabling geodatabase

The database we have designed is not geo-enabled, thus we cannot publish GIS services before we enable geodatabase on that database. To do that, we need a DBMS and an enterprise geodatabase, but we can also make it with a personal geodatabase.

 You must have Microsoft Office installed for ArcMap to connect to the Excel sheet.

Open **ArcMap**. From the main menu, click on **Add Data** and browse to the file
`Belize_landmarks.xls`, double-click on the file, and select the **Belize_Landmarks$**
sheet to add it to the map as shown in the following screenshot:

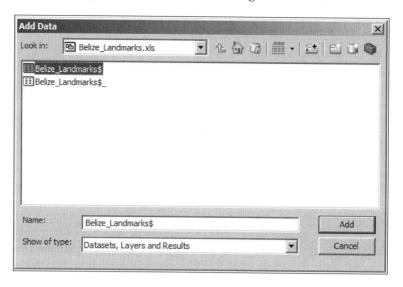

You can't exactly see anything yet on the map because this Excel sheet is just a table,
but fortunately, ArcMap can fix this. It can turn this mere table into a geo-enabled
feature class. To do that, right-click on the **Belize_Landmarks$** table in the **Table of
Contents** and click on **Display XY Data**.

Although what we have are not, in fact, the X and Y coordinates, they are longitude and latitude data. ArcMap already figured that out and selected them for you as you can see in the **Display XY Data** form. Just in case you didn't get that, from the **X Field** drop-down list, select the **Longitude** column and from the **Y Field** drop-down list, select the **Latitude** column. Now, we have to set the coordinate system. We will set it to Mexican Datum of 1993. Click on the **Edit** button and then expand **Geographic Coordinate System**. Then expand the **North America** node and select **Mexican Datum of 1993**. Click on **OK** to close the **Spatial Reference Properties** window and click on **OK** to accept the change. You might be prompted with a warning message saying that there is no ObjectID for the table. ArcMap needs it to keep track of each record so that it can simply generate its own field.

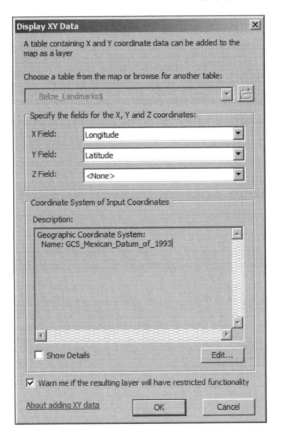

ArcMap will begin working on your table to display the longitude and latitude information on the map. Once this is done, you will see the map with the default symbology.

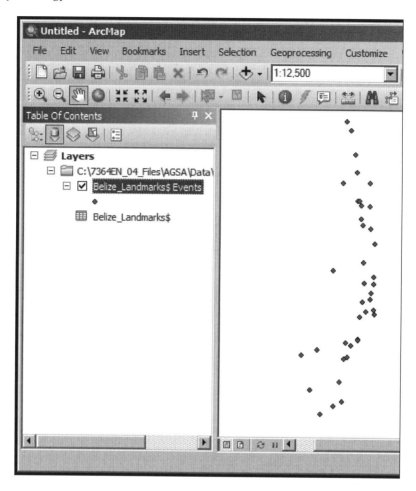

This is a good step, but it is still a table. It is not a geo-enabled object yet, so we need to export it with whatever changes we have made to the personal or file geodatabase. To do that, you can follow the given steps:

1. Right-click on the **Belize_Landmarks** layer from the **Table of Contents**, point to **Data**, and click on **Export Data** as shown in the following screenshot:

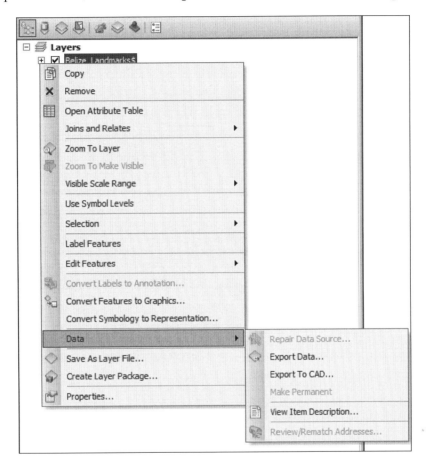

2. From the **Export** drop-down list, select **All Features** and in the output feature class field, click on the browse icon. This will ask you to select an existing geodatabase. Because we don't have one, we will create a temporary one.

3. First, browse to the file package `7364EN_04_Files\AGSA\Data` and from the **Saving Data** dialog, click on the New File Geodatabase icon on the left to create a new file geodatabase.

4. Name it `Belize` and then select it.

5. Name your feature class `Landmarks` and then click on **Save**. The new geodatabase won't appear unless the **Save as type** is set to **File and Personal Geodatabase feature classes**.

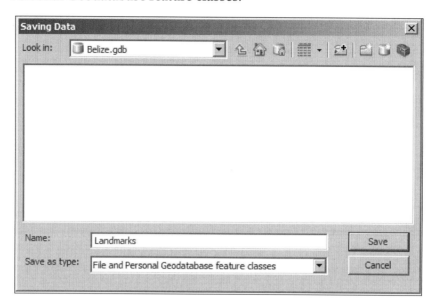

6. Click on **OK** to start exporting.

7. After the process is finished, ArcMap will ask if you want to add the new feature class to the map, click on **Yes**.

8. Uncheck the old table and leave the new layer checked.

You have successfully created a geodatabase out of Belize tabular format.

Best practice

It is recommended to move this feature class to an enterprise geodatabase of your choice, as we have designed in the UML deployment diagram.

Adding a world basemap

You will need some land cover information in order to visualize the landmarks and since the case study did not specify any, we will use ESRI world public service. To add the base map for the world data, you can use the REST URL `http://server.arcgisonline.com/ArcGIS/rest/services/World_Topo_Map/MapServer` and add it to your map. You can refer to the previous chapter for more details on this subject.

Authoring GIS services

Now that we have a geodatabase, you can use the skills you acquired in the previous chapters to implement this design. You can see how we drove through the case study, from the planning, analyzing, designing, and now to implementing the solution. You can practically apply these steps to all your projects. There are, however, a few things we need to do before you implement the design. The map document needs to be prepared and there is some work to do on that. Open a fresh ArcMap document and add your new `Landmarks` feature class from the Belize geodatabase. As you may have noted, this feature class contains all categories. We need to filter them and display only the Food and Drinks data. So, the first thing to do is rename the **Landmarks** layer to Foods and Drinks so that we don't get confused. Then, we need to apply a definition query, double-click on the **Foods and Drinks** layer to receive a pop up with its **Layer Properties** and activate the **Definition Query** tab. Type in the following query:

```
"Category" = 'Food and Drink'
```

To prevent errors, you may use the query builder, a tool in ArcMap that helps you build and verify SQL statements. This will only show those features that fall into the **Food and Drinks** category.

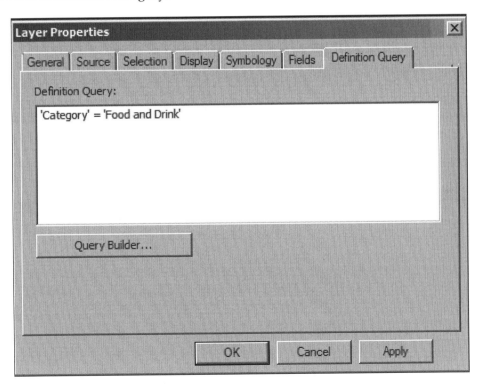

Use the **Symbology** tab to categorize by the **SubCategory** field and give each a related symbology icon. Make sure you use simple and straightforward symbologies for your layers; complex and 3D symbologies are not supported in Server yet. So, you should end up with something like the following:

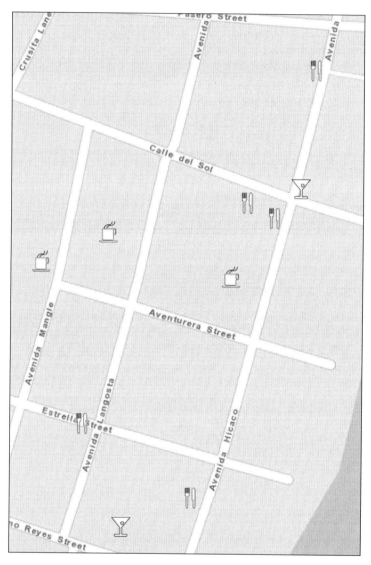

You should now remove the Esri world map because it cannot be published with your data. Now, publish this service and name it `Food_and_Drinks`. Remember, users should be able to query this service so they can search for their favorite dining place. So, we need to enable the query capability. From the **Service Editor** form, activate the **Mapping** tab and make sure the **Query** option is checked. Using the same technique used in option 1, you can implement the multiservice option. Similarly, in option 2, you just have to create three map documents.

TO-DO

Deploy option 2 using the same technique you learned in the previous chapters by authoring three services for each Restaurants, Bars, and Cafes. Then, draw the symbology for each service based on the **Rating** field instead.

Summary

Planning is of the essence, thinking ahead to what you want to accomplish with the GIS services can put you on the right track and save you time and resources. In this chapter, you learned how to analyze requirements and plan your GIS services. You then designed the nominated GIS services with UML tools. You also used an ER diagram to design the geodatabase that feeds the services. You eventually implemented your GIS services using the techniques you learned in the previous chapters. The skills you have acquired in this chapter will help you effectively plan a new ArcGIS for Server implementation. In the next chapter, you will learn new approaches for optimizing your ArcGIS to help the server run more efficiently.

5

Optimizing GIS Services

In the previous chapter, you learned how to analyze your requirements to plan ahead in order to move your geographic data as a service. You have acquired the skills necessary to design the GIS services into models that are ready to be deployed. With the toolset you acquired in the previous chapters, you know how to author and publish the services you design. You have learned how to consume these services from different end points. You have even written your own code to do that. Now that you've got the services up and running, it is time to manage them and make them run efficiently. After the GIS services are deployed, they usually start with a few megabytes of memory and as the consumption increases, the GIS server scoops out more and more memory for these services. Sadly, we have limited memory and processing power, so we have to distribute the GIS server's resources efficiently to those services that really need it.

In this chapter, you will learn three techniques in Server that you can apply to achieve interesting optimizing results. The first technique is **pooling**, where the running instances of your services are grouped in a pool. This way, each instance can be re-used several times thus serving more users. The second technique is **process isolation**, which helps you learn how these instances can be grouped into a single process or multiple processes to share resources. The final one you might be familiar with is **caching**, where the data gets stored locally on the GIS servers to save the expensive call to the database. You can control these pillars much like an equalizer to balance the efficiency of your services.

GIS service instance

Any service that you publish on ArcGIS for Server eventually gets compiled into one or more instances running on the GIS servers. They are distributed evenly throughout the GIS servers and the number of instances on each server can be configured when you publish the service. To manage these running instances in an efficient way, Esri has come up with new techniques that you will learn in the next sections.

Pooling

GIS services enabled the use of cross platforms between different environments. Now, they can be consumed by a variety of clients from different software. The classical one-to-one model of having a dedicated instance for each connection doesn't fit anymore. It was inefficient to have a new instance for every established connection; it is as if you are opening a new **ArcMap** document every time. The GIS services have high affinity, and they tend to consume processing and memory power rapidly, so there must be a way around it. Another model was required to be plugged into Server to manage more connections with the available limited resources. Therefore, Esri introduced the pooling technology into Server for the first time in 2007 and it was revolutionary. This model allows each connection to use a GIS service instance for a certain amount of time, which could span from milliseconds to minutes. Each instance can serve one connection at a time, for example, if one user is using ArcMap to zoom to an extent in a GIS service containing the world data, the new requested extent is sent to the Web server, which delegates the request to one of the GIS servers, which uses a free instance to execute the request. Depending on the request, the execution can take from milliseconds to minutes, and during this time the instance is labeled as busy. Once the execution is completed, the instance is released and the GIS server returns the result. This allows multiple connections to feed from one pool of instances. Using this technology, a single instance can serve up to 10 connections or even more depending on the usage.

The anatomy of pooling

To explain pooling better, let us say that we have an electric map service running on GIS-SERVER01. You can visualize this with the following diagram. Initially, as you can see, there is one instance running:

Let's assume there is a new request R1 to zoom to a new extent to see more power cables. This request is forwarded to GIS-SERVER01 to be executed as shown in the following diagram:

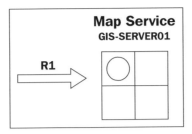

The GIS-SERVER01 finds that there is a free instance running and assigns R1 to this instance for execution as shown in the following diagram:

The R1 request is executed successfully. The instance is now free again for re-use. GIS-SERVER01 receives two more requests R2 and R3. They are network tracing requests, which take significantly more time to execute. There is one free instance now after executing R1 and there are no other new instances available. However, there is room to create new instances so the server assigns R2 to the first instance, and creates one more instance and assigns R3 to it, as shown in the following diagram:

Meanwhile, three more requests come at the same time: R4 and R5, which are again tracing requests, and R6 which is a zoom-in operation. There are no available free instances, the two available instances are busy executing R2 and R3, and so the server creates two additional instances, filling up the maximum number of instances for this GIS service. Unfortunately, there is no way for Server to predict the size of the request and how long it will take so it can assign resources efficiently, but we can hope for this feature in the future releases. The worst-case scenario is that R4 and R5 get the fresh instances and R6, which is a simple zoom operation, has to wait until a free instance is available. The maximum and minimum number of instances along with the wait time can all be configured as parameters while publishing the GIS service. Refer to the following diagram:

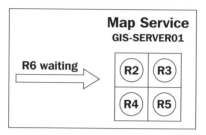

Esri kept the pooling approach optional until Version 10.1 when it was forced as a resource management technique while publishing any service. It was kept optional because of a limitation in the pooling technology. Pooling does not remember connection history, which means a pooled connection can use different instances each time a request is initiated. This also means editing could not keep track of edit logs or web editing workflow, hence no undo or redo operations are performed. Esri managed to find a way to enable editing on pooled services starting from the 10.1 architecture.

Configuring pooled services

You will now try configuring the pooling parameters for some of the services you published in the previous chapters. These parameters should be carefully selected based on the nature of the service, for example, if a service is not used frequently, you can minimize the number of its instances. Alternatively, if a service is busy or is likely to be used more frequently, you might want to increase the number of instances. Let us take the Parcels service that you have already published. This service is considered a **simple service** because there aren't many operations performed on Parcels. Users will only zoom and pan on Parcels features, unlike the Electricity service, where the user can run network analysis and complex operations. The Electricity service is an example of **rich services**. Let's try to edit the Parcels service and reconfigure the pooling parameters.

Open the **ArcGIS Server Manager** window and edit the `Parcels` service. Click on the pooling option from the list on the left-hand side. The **Minimum number of instances per machine** field shows the number of instances your services should start with. Currently it is 1, which means a single instance will run whenever you activate this service. Also note that it says "per machine", which means that this will be applied to each GIS server. So if I have two GIS servers, `GIS-SERVER01` and `GIS-SERVER02` configured on my Server site, I will have a single instance running on each server, which makes a total of two instances. Setting **Minimum number of instances per machine** to 2 will result in four instances. If I know that `Parcels` data are rarely queried in this context, meaning there is no need for it to occupy an instance at startup, I would change this parameter to 0. Don't worry! Whenever someone requests the `Parcels` service, a new instance will be created and the request will be fulfilled. Go ahead and set the minimum instances to 0. The second parameter is **Maximum number of instances per machine**. This field sets the threshold to the number of instances in a GIS service. Users of the service have to wait for a free instance if the maximum numbers of instances are all in use and no new instances will be created. You can set this parameter to 1, since there are no complex operations on the `Parcels` service and one instance can serve plenty of users. While the instance is busy serving a request, other users have to wait. Now, this wait time can also be configured in the **The maximum time a client will wait to get a service** field. It is currently set to a minute, which is quite a long time. It is better to reduce this time because we know that a zoom-in, zoom-out, or pan operation shouldn't take more than few seconds in worst cases. So change this parameter to 15 seconds. Any request that takes more than 15 seconds to be fulfilled should be discarded and requested again. This way we save more memory at the buffer at a slight cost of unsatisfying a few requests. Similarly, the field **The maximum time a client can use a service** is used to configure how long a client can consume an instance. We know that all operations on `Parcels` are simple and shouldn't take more than 5 seconds. Currently, it is set by default at 600 seconds, which is an average figure Esri came up with. The default value might be different depending on the version of Server. If a request takes more than that, it means something went wrong, perhaps a network failure, an infinite logic loop, and so on. Server can terminate the request and free the instance for other healthier requests. Any service that is not used for a long time should be removed from the memory to free up space for other services.

We could argue over what a long time really is, but in our example, `Parcels` are rarely queried and they consume a lot of memory due to their size. So instead of 30 minutes, I would set the **The maximum time an idle instance can be kept running** to 1 minute (60 seconds) as shown in the following screenshot:

Specify Number of Instances		
Minimum number of instances per machine:	0	
Maximum number of instances per machine:	2	
Specify Service Timeouts		
The maximum time a client can use a service:	5	seconds
The maximum time a client will wait to get a service:	15	seconds
The maximum time an idle instance can be kept running:	60	seconds

Best practice

Determine whether your service is simple or rich before configuration as this will help you set optimal pooling parameters.

Let us modify the pooling configuration for the `Electricity` service. Note that this service is more vital as we have called it a typical request that can take a significant amount of time to execute. It is not just a zoom operation, it could be tracing, network analysis, and many complex operations, therefore instances should be available at all times. As you can see in the following screenshot, I have increased the minimum and maximum instances. There must be at least one instance running and enough room for more instances. I have also increased the idle time to one hour, so even if the instance is idle, it should stay for an hour before it gets removed. We did that because it is expensive to create an instance. It takes time and we want to fulfill requests to this service in a responsive manner. The following screenshot shows the configuration we selected for the `Electricity` service:

Specify Number of Instances		
Minimum number of instances per machine:	1	
Maximum number of instances per machine:	4	
Specify Service Timeouts		
The maximum time a client can use a service:	60	seconds
The maximum time a client will wait to get a service:	60	seconds
The maximum time an idle instance can be kept running:	3600	seconds

Best practice
Never use the default pooling parameters on a production setup.
Always analyze the nature of your services and carefully set the pooling
parameters accordingly.

Process isolation

Process isolation is another optimization technique that controls the number
of GIS-service instances in a process. You can either perform high or low process
isolation and each has its merits. By having more instances in a single process,
you are performing a low-isolation technique. By lowering the number of
instances, you are spreading your instances into multiple processes, thus
performing a higher isolation. In Server, having a single instance in a
process is referred to as high isolation.

High-isolation configuration

By isolating each instance in a single process the instance will have its own dedicated
area in the memory heap. This means a service with high isolation is less likely
to experience downtime and failure. Even if a process is terminated or a memory
leakage happened in one of the processes, only one instance will be recycled
while the rest of the instances will remain available. Since each instance requires a
dedicated process in this approach, this will require more memory, thus your GIS
server should have more RAM to accommodate such configuration.

Services with high isolation techniques are more stable, but they require
more memory because each instance in a service reserves its own process.

Let us revisit the same example we used in the pooling topic, this time with high
isolation configuration. Initially, the `Electricity` GIS service has one minimum
instance running, which means in this configuration one process should be running.
In the following diagram, the rounded rectangle is the process and the circle is
the instance. Request `R1` comes and there is a free instance, so it is assigned to
it for execution:

Request R1 is completed and the instance is now free again for re-use. For requests R2 and R3, there is one free instance now after executing R1 and there are no other new instances available, so GIS-SERVER01 creates a new process to host a new instance as shown in the following diagram:

Meanwhile, R4, R5, and R6 are received while the server is busy executing R2 and R3. There are not enough instances, and so the server creates two more processes for the new requests. The R6 request has to wait for a free instance because according to the pooling configuration there is a maximum of four instances per server, as shown in the following diagram:

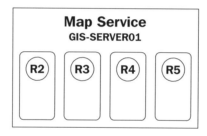

Low-isolation configuration

Low isolation configuration requires less memory as it groups multiple instances in a single process. These instances share the same allocated memory with their siblings in the same process. The downside of this approach is that when a process fails, all instances hosted by this process are withered.

 Services with low isolation techniques require less memory but they are more likely to become unavailable in the event of a process failure.

Let's see how a service with low isolation configuration of three instances per process behaves. The request R1 is received; there is a free instance to which it is assigned:

Request R1 is completed, R2 and R3 are received, R2 is assigned the free instance, and R3 has to have a new instance. The new instance is created in the same process, as shown in the following diagram:

While the server is busy executing R2 and R3, the requests R4, R5, and R6 are received. A new instance is created for R4. This fills out the first process and the server has to create a new process to host the new requests. The second process is created with a new instance to which R5 is assigned. Again, R6 has to wait since we are allowed to have a maximum of four instances. Notice that we have consumed less memory with this configuration. Refer to the following diagram:

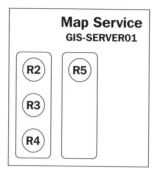

Configuring process isolation

Now that we know how the process isolation works, we need to learn how to configure it. Edit one of your services from the **ArcGIS Server Manager** window and click on the **Processes** tab. From **Specify Isolation Settings**, select **Low Isolation** or **High Isolation** depending on your preferences. If you however selected **Low Isolation**, you will notice that you can change the number of the **Instances per process** field, as shown in the following screenshot:

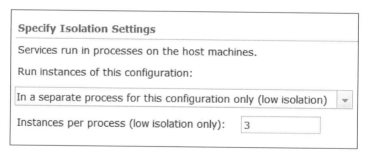

Recycling and health check

The operating system periodically runs diagnostics and analysis on the memory and does some modification on the data address such as defragmentation and other routine tasks to optimize the running processes. However, the OS does not maintain the internal part of an allocated memory, therefore, ArcGIS for Server provides you with the option to recycle process isolation configuration periodically so that the OS routine optimizing tasks can kick-in to help maintain performance and stability. You can change **Recycling Interval** from the **Processes** tab to recycle. Server also provides the option **Periodically check and repair data connections for idle instances**. It allows Server to periodically scan for idle instances and verify that they can still connect successfully to the database. I usually uncheck this option as it adds an extra cost on the GIS servers. The pooling configurations we specified earlier are enough to clear idle instances. If you do want to enable this option, make sure that this interval spans wide, over an hour, to avoid making unnecessary connections to the database. The following is the screenshot of the recycling configurations:

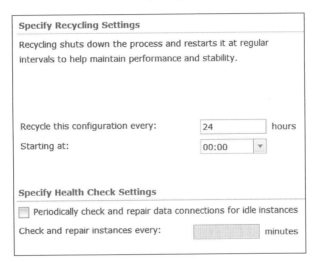

Specify Recycling Settings

Recycling shuts down the process and restarts it at regular intervals to help maintain performance and stability.

Recycle this configuration every: 24   hours
Starting at: 00:00

Specify Health Check Settings

☐ Periodically check and repair data connections for idle instances
Check and repair instances every: minutes

Best practice

It is more efficient to shut down an instance with idle connections instead of repairing it.

Caching

Caching is probably the most effective optimization tool to speed up the services' response time. When executing a particular request, the GIS server spends almost all of the execution time connecting to the database, indexing, querying, retrieving records, geoprocessing, projecting, and writing the map to an image, which is finally returned. You may notice that all these operations are database related. So if you could eliminate the database factor, you could save a huge amount of processing time. Here is where the concept of caching is introduced. If you could generate tiles of images for certain scales and store them locally on the GIS server's physical hard drive, you can simply index a request to a set of tiles and return them immediately without connecting to the database and doing all this overhead work. Caching could slash a big portion of processing time, minimizing the response time to more than 80 percent and consequently increasing successful requests or **throughput**. Not only can this optimize the service-request processing, it can also minimize the number of queries to the database to make it healthier and more responsive to other high priority queries. Caching doesn't come without flaws though. Saving images of different scales for different layers requires, well, storage. To do a good caching that is noticeable, you need at least 10 to 20 gigabytes of free disk space depending on the size of your database, and that is a lot. Moreover, if your data is frequently edited, you might not get much out of caching since your users will see an older version of the data, a cached version. Unless you update the cache frequently you will end up with an outdated service that is fast to load, but not very useful.

We will now create caching for the Building service. We don't have this service on our Server site yet, but we will author and publish it. Let us assume that you get the Buildings data on CDs on a yearly basis, where you then move them into your database. In this case, you can safely cache this data and use it for a year before you update it. It is efficient to create the Building cache to save database hits and speed up the loading process. Open **ArcMap** and browse to the Building feature class in 7364EN_05_Codes\AGSA\Data\Buildings.gdb and add it to the map. Change the symbology to the BuildingType category so that we can differentiate the types of buildings. We have done that previously so it should be an easy task. Now, we have to set the scale on which the building layer is visible. We will set the minimum scale to 1:4000; this means zooming out beyond 4000 — any scale number larger than 4000 — will render the building invisible.

To do that, double-click on the **Building** layer from the table of content and activate the **General** tab. Select **Don't show layer when zoomed**, type 4000 in the **Out beyond** field, and click on **OK**, as shown in the following screenshot:

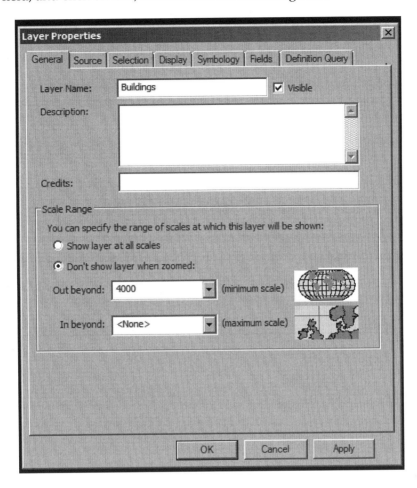

Go ahead and publish your new building document as a service. Refer to *Chapter 2, Authoring Web Services*, for detailed steps. From the **Service Editor** window, activate the **Caching** tab from the left-hand side and then select **Using tiles from a cache** to enable caching. The tiling scheme is the theme by which you want to cache your service. You can mimic an existing service such as Google Maps or you can create your own. Since we do not have any cached service, we will let Server suggest the tile scheme for us. Select **Suggest** from the **Tiling Scheme** drop-down list as shown in the following screenshot:

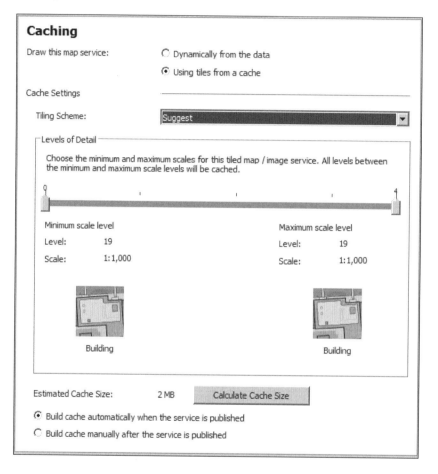

Open the **Advanced Settings** window. You will see that Server suggested four scale levels starting from **1000** going down to **125**. We need to add two more scale levels **2000** and **3000** and use the **Add** button to add the two scale levels. Note that Server calculates the disk space necessary for each scale level as well. Don't forget to register your database before you click on **Publish**. The following screenshot illustrates the different scale levels:

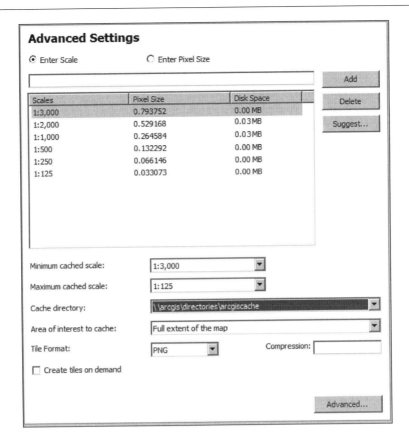

After publishing is completed, you will see a message indicating that your service has been published; however, the caching is still building. Caching is a long process and it requires sometime. GIS servers will be busy during caching so it is recommended that you do it during less busy hours. The screenshot for the **Service Publishing Result** message prompt is as follows:

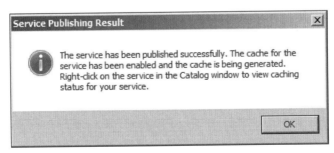

Another approach to building the cache for a service is through the **geoprocessing** tools. Although you can create and manage your cache from the **ArcGIS for Server Manager** window, I would advise you to do it from **ArcCatalog**, the reason being that caching takes a huge amount of time and consumes almost the entire memory. **ArcGIS for Server Manager** is a web interface, which runs on a browser unlike ArcCatalog, which is a standalone executable program that can withhold heavy operation. Start ArcCatalog and create an administrator connection to your Server site. Here is how you create an admin connection:

1. From **Catalog Tree**, expand the **GIS Servers** node.

2. Double-click on the **Add ArcGIS Server** node to add a new connection.

3. From the **Add ArcGIS Server** form, select **Administer GIS Server** and then click on **Next**.

4. In the Server URL, type in your server site address:
   `http://GIS-SERVER01:6080/arcgis`.

5. Type in the primary administrator **Username** and **Password** and click on **Finish**.

6. Rename the connection to `Admin@GIS-SERVER01`.

Activate the connection; you will see the list of all your services. Now, we need to open **ArcToolbox** and run the geoprocessing tool that will create the cache for us. From **ArcToolBox**, expand the **Server Tools** and **Caching** nodes to see the list of caching tools we have. Double-click on the **Create Map Service Cache** tool:

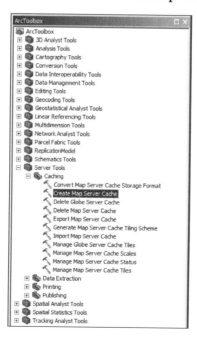

A new window will pop up. You will experience a similar look and feel when working with geoprocessing forms. Esri adopted the concept of model builders in the previous few releases of ArcGIS, and it is clearly planning to move its core functionality into geoprocessing tools. With this, users can re-use and mash these tools together to build bigger models. In the **Create Map Server Cache** form, you need to select the **Input Service** option you want to cache. You can use the **Browse** button or conveniently drag it from the catalog tree to the input box. The **Service Cache Directory** dialog box will be automatically populated. If you remember, you already configured that in the Server site back in *Chapter 1, Best Practices for Installing ArcGIS for Server*, ArcGIS for Server populates it for you. This folder is basically the output of the caching operation where the cache is stored. Next are the scales. It is not feasible to create cache for all scales as this will require unlimited space. Cache has to be created for certain scales: the busy scales which are asked for frequently. Server helps you analyze your service and recommend certain scales to cache, for example, it is pointless to cache scales on which layers are invisible. Select **New** for **Tiling Scheme** and **Standard** for **Scale Type**, and in the **Number of Scales** field type 3. Server will suggest three different scales. Leave the rest of the options to default and click on **OK**. You should see the following prompt message when the tool finished running:

If you are planning to cache more services, it might be a good idea to create your own template tiling scheme and then apply it on the new service. In this template, there is an XML file that contains the default scales, image **Dot per Inch** (**DPI**), compression, tile size, and other parameters. You can generate the tiling scheme file using the **Generate Tile Cache Tiling Scheme** tool from **ArcToolBox**. Then you can use the XML tile scheme to enable caching from the **Server Editor** while creating or editing the service.

Best practice

Planning the scales you want to cache is crucial. You have to see at what scales your service gets busy, and cache those scales accordingly.

Summary

If there was unlimited memory and processing power, you wouldn't have to optimize your GIS services and I wouldn't have written this chapter. However, unfortunately, we do have limited resources and we have to use them efficiently to get our services to run comfortably. In this chapter, you have learned a number of approaches to optimize your ArcGIS for Server. You now know that careful planning and analysis is required to select the correct parameters and preferences that will make your Server run at its optimal state. The techniques you learned, namely pooling, process isolation, and caching are sufficient, if used as guided, to bring the most out of your ArcGIS for Server and make your GIS services run much more efficiently and effectively. In the next chapter, you will be introduced to the clustering technique. This will help you group and categorize your GIS servers in order to use them more effectively.

6
Clustering and Load Balancing

One of the vital features of ArcGIS for Server is load balancing. How a GIS server can take over in case others are busy or highly loaded is certainly a very important aspect of maintaining good response time. When a request is made to consume a GIS service, the Web server (whether dedicated or built in) keeps logs in the Server site. These include which GIS server is free and which one is not. The decision regarding which GIS server should get this request next is made accordingly. The server then executes the request efficiently using the optimization tools we discussed in *Chapter 5, Optimizing GIS Services*. The load balancing module is a closed box, which means you get to enjoy the experience of Server balancing the requests between your GIS servers but cannot peek under the hood and configure it. It would be really useful if Esri were to expose this part for us to play with; it did, however, enable us to tap into something really interesting — **clustering**.

In this chapter, we will discuss clustering technology, which has its benefits and limitations. By implementing clustering, you will see how easy it is to scale up a Server site and add machines. You will know how to group and categorize GIS servers based on their characteristics to ensure proper load balancing on your Server site. Despite its advantages, clustering does come with some limitations that we will discuss as well.

Clustering

For any service you publish on ArcGIS for Server, one or more instances will start on the GIS servers to represent that service. Each instance takes resources from the machine it is running on. The number of instances on each server can be configured when you publish the service. Each GIS service differs in terms of memory usage and processing consumption, and the same thing applies on the GIS servers. You might have different generations of servers with different specs and resources, so it makes sense to have some sort of distribution window by which you can specify which services will run on which servers. To manage this in an efficient way, Esri came up with a technique to group GIS servers into clusters and then permit you to configure which service goes to which cluster of machines. Clustering is an advanced technique that can prove to be of use if configured correctly. For instance, you have some unused workstations or some standard-issue PCs lying around in your inventory that you can format; make them fresh and ready, add them to your Server site, and place them into a **commodity computing** cluster. You can then assign those services with low priority to run on this cluster and free up your more powerful GIS servers to host services with higher affinity. Within a cluster, the GIS servers need to communicate with each other and update each other with vital information to help in the load balancing process. This communication happens using the **Transmission Control Protocol (TCP)** by default on a unique port. Each cluster gets assigned a dedicated port, and if there are any firewalls in place, that port on which the GIS servers communicate must be opened or an exception must be added to the firewall rules to allow the servers to exchange information freely.

Commodity computing

Commodity computing is the use of a large number of available, average-power machines into a cluster to obtain high computing power at a lower cost.

Creating clusters

Before you start creating clusters, you have to determine what type of GIS services you possess. This is done by properly planning and designing GIS services, analyzing their nature, and predicting what kind of resources are required, which you have already done back in *Chapter 4, Planning and Designing GIS Services*. Once you identify your GIS services, you can decide what kind of clusters you want to create. You might not require any clustering at all; however, sometimes you need to group your GIS servers by some factors. GIS services can be grouped by resources and computing power, where you put the most resourceful GIS servers into one cluster and your typical ones in another cluster.

You can group your servers by security level; you can assign high-profile and sensitive GIS services running on servers with tightened cyber and physical security to a dedicated cluster. Some even create clusters by networking area, where servers within the same area network and subnet are grouped together and remote servers are put into a separate cluster. Of course, there is always the ownership factor to consider; you can group servers by owner, making them easily manageable.

Take a look at the following network diagram: there are two high-power servers — `GIS-SERVER01` and `GIS-SERVER02` — connected directly to the database that hosts the GIS data — `SDE-SERVER01`. Another five PCs — `GIS-PC01` to `GIS-PC05` — are connected to the database via a 1 Gbps Ethernet, and finally, to one powerful, cloud VPN-leased server — **GIS-REMOTE01** — in China with a 42 Mbps Internet bandwidth.

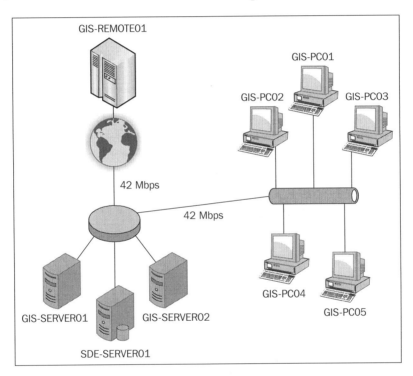

All these eight GIS servers are joined to an ArcGIS for Server site and are load balanced. You have four services running on the Server site: Building, Parcels, Electricity, and Geoprocessing. Users are frequently experiencing slow performance on the overall services despite the high-spec configuration and networking setup, and the management is not happy to hear this, especially after spending a large sum of money purchasing and leasing servers. You were asked to solve the slow performance problem by first identifying the cause of the problem. On looking, you will find that load balancing is not intelligent enough to take into consideration the resources and networking factors. For example, if you run a geoprocessing task, you might get diverted to one of the commodity PCs, which are not designed for such tasks. To prevent this, the first thing we need to do is to create clusters for our machines and put each machine in the right cluster.

Log in to your ArcGIS Server Manager, activate the **Site** tab, and from the left-hand pane, click on **Clusters**. By default, there is always one cluster — **default** — which is created when you set up your Server site, and all the machines are placed into this cluster. Manager looks as follows:

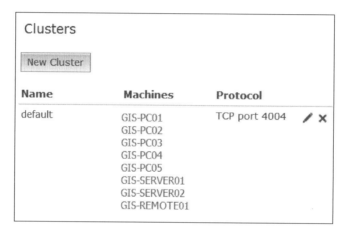

Adding machines to the default cluster

First, we need to create a new cluster for the five PCs. Click on **New Cluster**, and in the **New Cluster** form, type Commodity Computers in the **Cluster Name** field. You will notice that all the available machines get listed in the **Machines** box. In this case, you might not see any machine, and that is ok, since they are already assigned to another cluster **default**. Click on **Create** to add the new cluster. The **New Cluster** form now looks as follows:

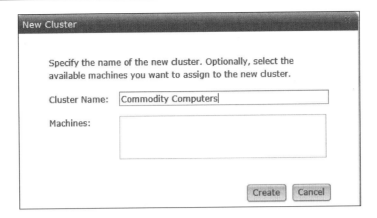

Note that there are no machines registered on your new cluster, and this is expected because you didn't add any machine to this cluster yet. That is why we need to rearrange the machines. To do that, we need to edit the **default** cluster; we will show how to do this in a while. Our **Clusters** form now looks as follows:

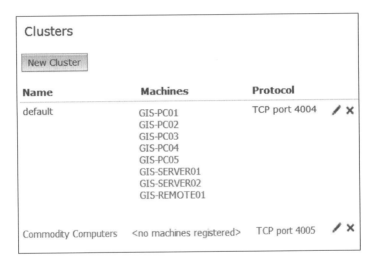

Grouping machines by resources

Now that all machines are added to the default cluster, we need to group them into separate cluster by their resources, as we discussed earlier. **Commodity Computers** represents the five PCs that are already assigned to the **default** cluster: we need to remove those machines from the **default** cluster and assign them to the **Commodity Computers** cluster. To start editing the cluster, click on the edit icon next to the **default** cluster. In fact, let us remove all GIS servers from the **default** clusters and turn them into available machines so that we can easily assign them later.

From the **Added Machines** list, remove all servers, add them into the **Available Machines** list, and then click on **Apply**. The **Edit Cluster Machines** page looks as shown in the following screenshot.

Best practice

It is a good idea to implement clustering if you have three or more GIS servers on your Server site.

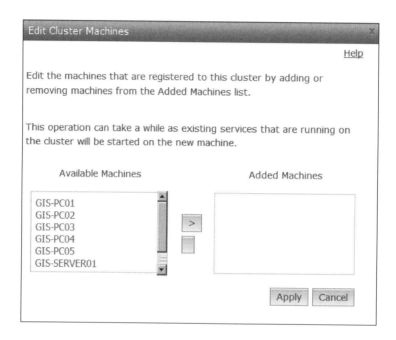

Note that the default cluster no longer has any machines, and now that the machines are free, we can reassign them to other clusters. Now the **Clusters** page appears as follows:

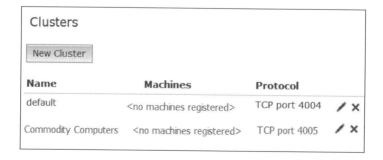

Go ahead and edit the **Commodity Computers** cluster, and move the five PCs from the **Available Machines** list to the **Added Machines** list by using the arrow icon. Click on **Apply** when you finish as shown in the following screenshot:

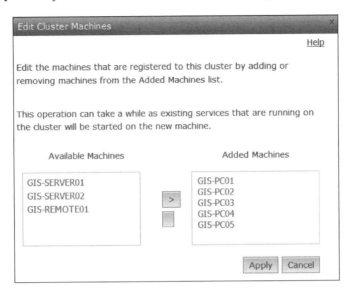

Usually the process of moving GIS servers from one cluster to another can take a long time, especially if there are existing services running on those servers, as they need to be restarted on each cluster. Various clusters can be seen as shown in the following screenshot:

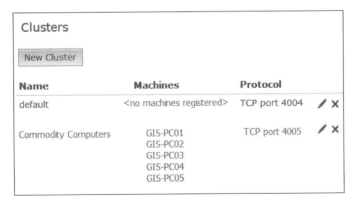

We will not require the **default** cluster anymore, so you can delete it; however, there are other system services, such as publishing and caching, that were using that cluster, and we have to reassign them as well to your new cluster. In the next topic, you will learn how to reassign a service to a new cluster. If you do not want to change your system services, keep the **default** cluster and assign one powerful machine to it.

This cluster is now up and running, hosting five GIS servers standard PCs, so we must be careful to assign services that are low priority and often queried to this cluster. It could even be used for testing GIS services. If you want to publish a new service but you want to test how it performs, you can first run it on the commodity cluster, and then after you see it is fine, you can decide whether to keep it or migrate it to a more powerful cluster. We will discuss about an application in the next topic. Now we need to create two more clusters. According to our network diagram, we have three more machines left; one is remote and is hosted externally and connected to the Internet, and the other two are local with a direct connection to the database. Logically, the remote server should go to a separate cluster for obvious reasons; security is one of them, control and management another. The rest of the servers are powerful pieces of hardware and they have high bandwidth connections to the database, so they are gems to us. We can put them in a new cluster called the **Power** cluster. Go ahead and create the **Power** and **Remote** clusters and assign **GIS-SERVER01** and **GIS-SERVER02** to the **Power** cluster and **GIS-REMOTE01** to the **Remote** cluster. After doing this, the **Clusters** form looks as follows:

Clusters

New Cluster

Name	Machines	Protocol		
Commodity Computers	GIS-PC01 GIS-PC02 GIS-PC03 GIS-PC04 GIS-PC05	TCP port 4005	✎	✗
Power	GIS-SERVER01 GIS-SERVER02	TCP port 4006	✎	✗
Remote	GIS-REMOTE01	TCP port 4007	✎	✗

Mapping GIS services to a cluster

We managed to set up three clusters of machines and took our network diagram and extracted a clustering pattern out of it. We then created the clusters and assigned the machines to those clusters based on different factors: resources, network cost, and locality. That was one side of the coin. We should now assign services to each cluster, and since you have multiple clusters, you will be asked to select which cluster you want to publish your GIS service on. To do this, we should first analyze the nature of the service, see how it behaves, and accordingly select the right environment for it. We have four services that we need to manage and map to clusters: **Parcels**, **Buildings**, **Electricity**, and **extraction geoprocessing**.

Mapping a simple map service

The **Parcels** service consists of only simple operations, such as pan and zoom and search, functions that seemingly do not require massive resources. It looks like it is a waste of resources to assign the **Power** or **Remote** cluster to such services; commodity computers can take care of this service easily.

> You may decide to cache this service; however, hosting it on the commodity cluster will be expensive as the whole cache need to be copied on all the five PCs. The next section covers the mapping of cached service.

To assign a service to a cluster, you can do it either from the **Service Editor** form or from the ArcGIS Server Manager. Open Manager and edit the **Parcels** service. From the left-hand pane, select **Parameters**, and then select **Commodity Computers** from the cluster drop-down list. Click on **Save** to save your changes. The changes will be as shown in the following screenshot:

Mapping a cached map service

The second service is **Buildings**, a service with an extensive number of features. The fact that this service is queried frequently made us decide to cache it so that we can save expensive calls to the database. You can imagine that plenty of space is required for caching, especially if you are going to implement it on many scales. Let us examine our clusters again. They are as follows:

- **Remote** cluster: Here I have a leased a powerful server set on a VPN connection over the Internet with a bandwidth of 42 Mbps

- **Power** cluster: It has two resourceful servers setting right on my 1 Gbps local area network connected directly to my database

- **Commodity** cluster: It has a set of five good workstations offering us their CPU cycles

Now, which one of these three clusters do you think is suitable to host our **Buildings** GIS service? That would definitely be the **Remote** cluster. The service does not require a database connection as it is cached. Since I'm renting this server, I can put the terabytes of disk space to good use by caching this service. It doesn't matter how far this remote server is because it won't require connecting to my database. Thus, all bandwidth will be used to download cached images only, which are PNG compressed files and are therefore fast to fetch.

To assign a service to a cluster, you can do it either from Service Editor or from the ArcGIS Server Manager. Open the manager and edit the **Buildings** Service. From the left-hand pane, select **Parameters**, and then select **Remote** from the cluster drop-down list as shown in the following screenshot. Click on **Save** to save your changes.

Once we map the **Buildings** service to the **Remote** cluster, all the cache will be created initially on the remote server; this process is long and will consume some time. As discussed in the previous chapter, it is recommended to run this overnight or when the database is less busy. You can also create the cache locally and upload it to the remote server. Either way, the advantage of this mapping is that you took a very busy service and managed to run it very efficiently and remotely without depleting your own resources. The folks at your finance department will be very happy to learn that you are fully utilizing the rented overseas server. The disadvantage of this is that you are overexposing your data remotely and insecurely; anyone could tap into the channel and copy these images and get access to your data. There is always a physical route by which your remote server can get infiltrated from the inside and your data get stolen.

Mapping a high-affinity map service

Let us take the third service, **Electricity**. This service is not requested very often, but when it is requested, it is always a complex request—a trace task that involves tapping into the geometric network and traversing downstream or upstream assets. Such requests require powerful machines; unfortunately, they cannot be cached because the data is dynamic and changing. It requires constant communication with the database. The **Commodity** cluster obviously wouldn't work; it is not powerful enough to handle such requests for this service. We can assign it to the **Remote** cluster just like **Buildings**, but we will have a bottleneck due to limited network bandwidth and latency. Establishing communication with the database over a VPN network makes the latency factor go very high, which consequently makes the service perform atrociously. The **Power** cluster seems to be the one that can handle this. We tried to use low-cost solutions to outsource CPU cycles and resources, but this service requires a resourceful server running on a local, high-bandwidth network right next to the database server. Go ahead and assign the **Electricity** service to the **Power** cluster as shown in the following screenshot:

Mapping a geoprocessing service

The last service is an extraction geoprocessing service that is developed to query the database and extract a user-defined boundary for the data. You're probably thinking that this is a very bandwidth-heavy service; this is true, and there will be a massive transfer of raw data. Plus, you require a powerful machine capable of crunching and processing this data. Therefore, the **Remote** cluster definitely cannot handle such a service although it is powerful. The fact that it is hosted over a 42 Mbps network excludes it as an option to serve our geoprocessing service. You can run it on the **Commodity** cluster since they are on the same network as the database is and this makes it a good candidate. However, if a geoprocessing job is received, it will assign the entire job to one of the commodity PCs, and that average-power PC will struggle with the job by itself. It might be able to pull it off eventually, but it will take a significant amount of time.

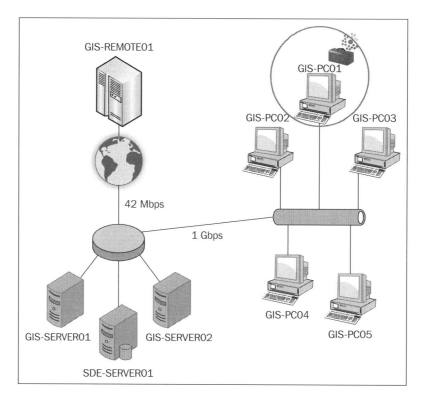

However, if this geoprocessing request were divided into blocks and then executed on a group of machines in parallel, just like **Hadoop** architecture, it would definitely make sense to assign it to the **Commodity** cluster.

Hadoop
Hadoop is an open source framework for large storage and high processing using commodity computing clusters.

Unfortunately, Server does not work this way, which leaves us with the **Power** cluster as the best candidate to map this geoprocessing service to.

Good job! You have managed to fix the performance problem on this ArcGIS for Server setup by properly balancing requests across the GIS Servers. The users are experiencing a great performance boost, thanks to your newly acquired skills.

If you have deleted the default cluster and you are faced with problems publishing your services, make sure that your system services in the ArcGIS Manager are running and assigned to a working cluster. Remember that system services need to be close to the database and need to run on powerful machines.

Scaling clusters

You have finished your initial ArcGIS for Server setup and determined your GIS Servers, GIS services, and clusters. Now, your users are increasing and the initial configuration does not support the increase in the volume of requests. This is when you need to decide whether you want to scale a cluster by adding more machines. The good news is that, once your clusters are created, they can scale very easily. Adding a GIS server to a cluster is simple: all you have to do is install ArcGIS for Server on the new machine that you want to add to the cluster and then join the machine to the Server site, which we have learned back in *Chapter 1, Best Practices for Installing ArcGIS for Server*. If you have a single cluster on your Server site, the new machine will directly be added to that default cluster. However, if your Server site has multiple clusters, you will be prompted to select one. It is important to mention that by scalability we mean adding physical machines and not virtual machines; this gives you more computing power from each machine. Adding virtual machines to a cluster will not give you any added value.

To add a machine to a cluster, install the GIS server component on your new machine and launch the ArcGIS Manager; you will be notified to either create a new Server site or join an existing one, as shown in the following screenshot. The URL for Manager is `http://GIS-SERVER04:6080/arcgis/manager`, where `GIS-SERVER04` is the new machine you want to join.

Click on **Join Existing Site** to attach the machine to your site and type in your Server site URL; remember that any machine that is joined to the Server site will point you to the Server site. Specify the username and password for the primary administrator account and click on **Next** as shown in the following screenshot.

 If you have any problem connecting to the Server site, use the IP address instead and make sure that you can ping the server and that port `6080` is allowed to receive connections on the firewall.

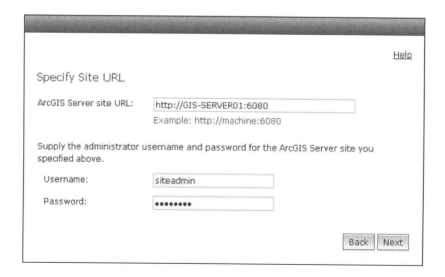

Since the Server site has more than one cluster, you will be prompted to select an existing cluster in order to join this machine. The machine will then be added to that cluster. Select the cluster and then click on **Next** as shown in the following screenshot.

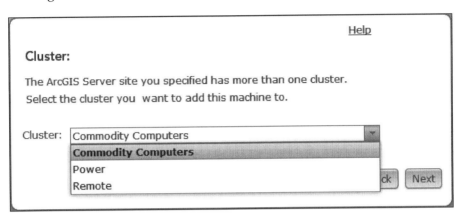

 As we discussed earlier, any cluster you select communicates through a TCP port, and that port should be opened for the information to flow in and out of each machine on that cluster. If that port is closed, you will not be able to join the cluster.

That is all. You will now get a summary of your configuration as a confirmation as shown in the following screenshot; click on **Finish** to join the Server site.

Best practice

Make sure to allow all cluster ports on all your GIS server firewalls before joining them; this will save you a huge amount of work. If you have a domain-level firewall, it will be easier to configure.

Limitations

Unfortunately, adding more machines to a cluster doesn't mean better performance. Yes, it can yield response time; however, the time for executing a particular request for a service will remain the same. That is because the request will be piped to a single machine (eventually), and that machine is responsible for fetching the required data from the database—be it a few records or thousands—and solely processing them. Distributed computing architectures, such as Hadoop, help utilize the power of parallel processing for all the machines by breaking up the data into parts and distributing them into cluster machines to be processed in parallel using the **MapReduce** concept. The power of Hadoop resides in the concept of **data locality**, where the database is accessed once and the result is fetched, divided into parts, and distributed to each machine for processing. Machines, in this case, do not need to query the database and this prevents networking latency. Instead, they work on the data locally on the disk, which gives a huge performance boost. I would like to see Esri implement Hadoop one day as its clustering platform; this will be a breakthrough in the GIS industry.

MapReduce

MapReduce is a programming model for processing large amounts of data on a group of machines using the concept of data locality. The model consists of two functions: **Map**, which filters the input, removes unnecessary things, and prepares the results, and **Reduce**, which performs the actual work and summarizes on the filtered results.

Another limitation is that having too many clusters can threaten security since you will be poking a lot of holes into your firewall to enable the communication between the machines. You will end up with a vulnerable sponge system, full of holes and very attractive prey to hackers.

Summary

In this chapter, you have learned a new technique ArcGIS for Server offers; clustering can be useful if used with caution and on the right GIS servers. You now know how to create a cluster from the Server site, where these clusters define the spectrum of your GIS servers. You have learned that clustering can be categorized by the machine power or memory or even by networking factors. You have learned how to assign a service to a cluster of machines so that its instances run only on those machines. You also know the limitations of clustering: what it can or can't do and when to use it.

In addition to the Server site optimization skills you acquired in the previous chapter, you now know how to take advantage of individual machines and organize them so that they perform more effectively. There are, of course, other factors that affect Server, but they are outside the scope of this book.

In the next chapter, we move from optimizing to securing ArcGIS for Server, where you will learn how to protect your GIS services from unauthorized access.

7
Securing ArcGIS for Server

Data, information, and applications are the digital assets of an organization. As these pillars expand and are deployed across different nodes, communication between these nodes becomes vital, and with communication comes the risk of compromising the data exchanged in the process. Thus, securing data and the means of networking are an essential part of any product. Authentication is not only a security measure, but also a necessary feature. Making sure that no one can tap into the data unless permitted to is one of the critical requirements for a product. In the previous chapter, we implemented the clustering technique that helped distribute GIS services evenly across machines so that they run effectively. However, it is important as well to make sure that these GIS services are properly secured against unauthorized access. ArcGIS for Server depends heavily on networking, so your data can be delivered and consumed as GIS services. The silver lining is that there is a good set of security mechanisms that can be configured to protect your GIS services. There are two tiers that can be configured for authentication and security, the **GIS server tier** and **web server tier**. The GIS-tier is the built-in tier managed by ArcGIS for Server and uses the ArcGIS token technology for authentication, while the Web-tier leverages your dedicated Web server authentication mechanisms. In this chapter, we will learn how to secure ArcGIS for Server using these methods.

User and role stores

Before we get into defining the GIS-tier and the Web-tier, we should first discuss the user and role stores. To provide proper data and network security, ArcGIS for Server must identify requests that are made to the GIS services. This is done by cross-referencing a user with the roles granted to that user. By doing so, Server can authenticate requests and allow or deny access to the subject GIS service according to the assigned roles. To achieve that, Server requires two tables, the **Users** and **Roles** tables. Configuring these tables or stores can be done either by manually populating the users and roles stores, where the stores will be maintained by Server, or linking it to the Windows domain. We will discuss how to do this in the coming pages.

GIS server tier – ArcGIS token security

The ArcGIS for Server token method is a built-in security mechanism to authenticate requests made to the GIS services. Esri had to develop their own authentication method in order to not be dependent on an existing preparatory product. Here is how it works:

1. The client makes a request to consume a GIS service.

2. ArcGIS for Server prompts for the username and password.

3. The client supplies the credentials and then Server verifies that against the user store.

4. If the username and password are valid, the Server combines the username, the password, and the expiration period of the token, and applies the **Advanced Encryption Standard (AES)** along with a shared key to encrypt all that into a string, which is known as a **token**.

5. The token is then appended to each request until it expires.

The following diagram shows the entire process:

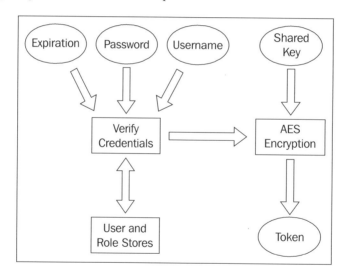

There are two types of tokens, **short-lived** and **long-lived**. The short-lived tokens have a relatively shorter expiration period; these are created by default if the expiration period is not specified while attempting to generate a token. Validity for short-lived tokens is measured in minutes, while that for long-lived tokens is measured in days. Since short-lived tokens expire quickly, they are more secure than long-lived tokens; however, this option requires the client to authenticate more frequently, which might become annoying in a less secure environment.

Enabling the ArcGIS token security

To configure ArcGIS for Server security to use the ArcGIS tokens and the built-in stores, log in to ArcGIS for Server Manager using your primary administrator account and then click on the **Security** tab as shown in the following screenshot:

On the **Configuration Settings** page, perform the following steps:

1. Click on the pen icon to start editing the security settings.

2. On the **Security Configuration Wizard** screen, choose **Users and roles from ArcGIS Server's built-in store**; this way, the users and roles will be managed by ArcGIS for Server, which means you have to add and maintain them manually.

3. Click on **Next**.

4. Click on **Finish** on the summary window.

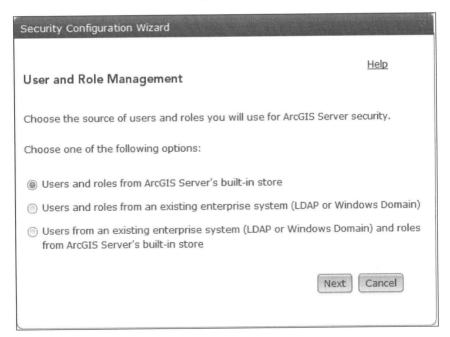

On the **Configuration Settings** page as shown in the following screenshot, you will see your new security settings. **User Store**, which is the user table that contains all the GIS users, and **Role Store**, which is the role table that contains the different roles configured in your ArcGIS for Server, are both using ArcGIS Server's built-in store. The **Authentication Tier** and **Authentication Mode** settings are set to use ArcGIS token on the GIS-tier.

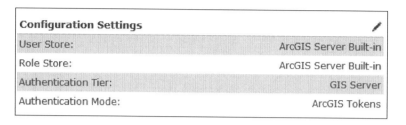

Adding new users and roles

You have now configured your Server security to use a token, but we still have more work to do; we don't have any users or roles, so we are going to create some. Under the **Security** tab, activate the **Users** tab to view the user identity store; there are no apparent users, so go ahead and click on **New User** as shown:

In the **New User** form, type gisuser01 in the **Username** field, choose a password, and an e-mail address. Note that there is a box for the roles; this is empty since we don't have any roles now, but it is there in order to assign the role directly as we create the user. Click on **Create** as shown in the following screenshot:

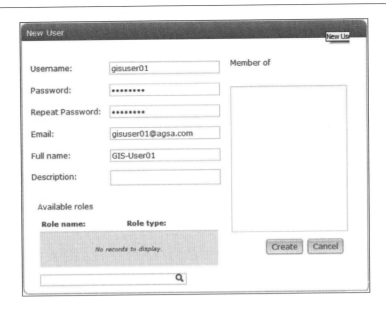

Now we have to add a new role and assign it to the user we just created; click on the **Roles** tab under **Security**, and then click on the **New Role** button as shown in the following screenshot:

In the **New Role** form, type View_Parcels in the **Role Name** field and type Ability to view the parcels service in the **Description** field. This is where it gets interesting. There are three types of roles: **Administrator**, **Publisher**, and **User**. The **Administrator** is a role that grants full administrator privileges to the Server site: users with the administrator role type can do whatever the primary administrator can do. There is the publisher role type, which gives the granted users the ability to publish services. The last one is the user role type, which is a custom role used by applications and the one we are going to select. From the **Role type** radio buttons, select **User**. You will see the user we just created—gisuser01—in the list below; click on the plus sign beside the user to assign it to the role.

Click on **Create** to save as shown in the following screenshot:

Enabling security on GIS services

Although we have configured the security on ArcGIS for Server, we haven't explicitly enabled any security or authentication mechanisms on our services. Services are public by default and can be accessed by any client. We have to set security for each GIS service by assigning a set of roles to the service. Let us go to our **Parcels** service and enable the security so that only people with the **View_Parcels** role can view this service. To do that, log in to ArcGIS for Server Manager, go to **Services**, and take a look at the **Parcels** service. You will notice the unlocked icon representing unsecured GIS services as shown in the following screenshot; this means it is available to anyone.

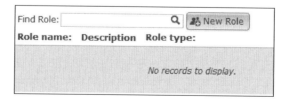

To edit the service security, click on the open lock icon; you will be prompted with the **Edit Permissions** form, where the default security setting is set to **Public, available to everyone**. Change that to **Private, available only to selected users** and then add **View_Parcels** to the roles of the service. A service with no roles assigned can only be viewed by administrators and publishers; this, of course, includes the primary site administrator. The **Edit Permissions** form now looks as follows:

You have to be careful who you give the publisher role to, because they can view, edit, and delete all kinds of services. An interesting idea on this subject has been discussed on ArcGIS Ideas. The topic suggests adding different admin levels to the ArcGIS for Server roles to allow more diversity in security. The topic can be found at `http://bit.ly/JUvJhW`; you may log in and vote on the idea.

> You can only assign security roles to a service. To allow a single user to read a service, you have to create a role, add that user to that role, and assign the role to the service. This makes configuration easier as it allows multiple users by adding those users to the roles without reconfiguring the services.

Connecting to a secured service

We will now connect to the secured service we just published from ArcMap. Since this service is secured, we will need to specify the username and password to establish the connection. Do you remember how to establish a connection to the service Site from ArcMap? Open ArcMap and make sure the **ArcCatalog** window is displayed by clicking on the **Windows** menu and then choose **Catalog**. Expand the **GIS Servers** node and double-click on **Add ArcGIS Server**. Since we will be consuming a new service, choose the **Use GIS services** option and click on **Next**. In the **General** form, type your **Server URL** address; you will now find two fields we usually keep empty in the **Authentication** frame: **User Name** and **Password**. It is time for you to use which user wants to connect to the server. We will use `gisuser01` for this purpose as shown in the following screenshot:

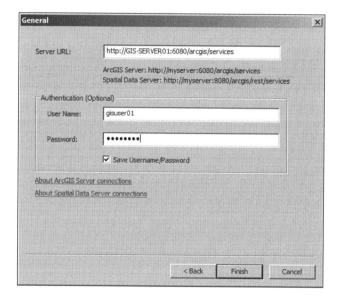

Click on **Finish** to create the connection and rename the connection to `gisuser01@ GIS-SERVER01`, depending on the server you have used.

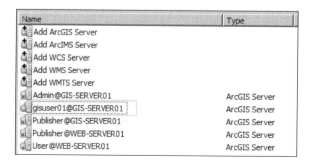

Double-click on the new connection and drag the **Parcels** GIS service to the map to add it; you won't feel much of a difference in performance, but your parcels layer is now authenticated, and only admins, publishers, and gisuser01 can see it. To test this, jump to ArcGIS for Server Manager and create a new user—gisuser02—don't assign him any roles yet. Try to reconnect, this time with gisuser02; as shown in the following screenshot. You will notice that you cannot see the **Parcels** service.

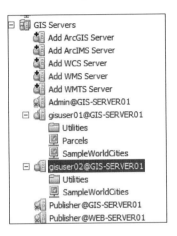

Similarly, you could access secured resources through code and the server will prompt you for credentials. Back in *Chapter 3, Consuming GIS Services*, we managed to connect to a GIS service using an ArcGIS JavaScript API; when the service you are about to consume is secured, the Server responds with the question "Who are you? Please enter your username and password." Let us use this code to achieve that; this is an OnlineMode example, so you will need the Internet to execute it. From the supporting files in 7364EN_07_Files\AGSA\Code, open the OnlineMode.html file. The content of the file are as follows:

```html
<html>
  <header>
    <scriptsrc="http://js.arcgis.com/3.5/"></script>

    <link rel="stylesheet"
      href="http://js.arcgis.com/3.5/js/dojo/dijit/themes/claro/claro.
css">

    <script>

    dojo.require("esri.map");

    functionstartup()
    {
```

```
    var map = new esri.Map("MapCanvas");

    var layer = new
      esri.layers.ArcGISDynamicMapServiceLayer("http://GIS-
        SERVER01:6080/arcgis/rest/services/Parcels/MapServer");

    map.addLayer(layer);

  }

  dojo.addOnLoad(startup);

  </script>
 </header>
 <body>

  <div id ="MapCanvas" style = "height: 100%;width:100%" ></div>

 </body>
</html>
```

If you compare this file with the one you have in *Chapter 3, Consuming GIS Services*, you will see this additional style file added. This file is required for the styling of the form which will ask you to enter the username and password. The additional code part is as follows:

```
<link rel="stylesheet"
  href="http://js.arcgis.com/3.5/js/dojo/dijit/themes/claro/claro.
css">
```

If you run the file, you will be prompted to enter the username and password because you are trying to access a secured resource. The prompt looks like this:

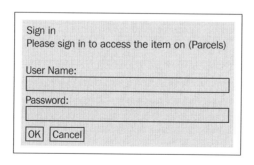

Using `gisuser01` will grant access to the resource; however, if you are planning to connect to the resource implicitly, you might want to consider another piece of code if you don't want to bore the user with prompts. This, of course, generates a short-lived token and it will be lost when you refresh the page.

Shared key security

A shared key is a string used to securely generate the token. Since AES—the method used for encryption in Server—is a symmetric-key encryption algorithm, this key is used to both encrypt and decrypt information. This means that if someone managed to get hold of this key, he/she could intercept and decipher the token, acquiring the username and password in plain text. That is why changing the shared key is a good practice to prevent such cases. You can change the shared key along with the lifespan of the tokens from ArcGIS for Server Manager. From the **Security** tab, edit **Token Settings** by clicking on the pen icon. Change them based on how high you want your security level.

Best practice

Make sure to change the shared key regularly to provide sustainable security.

Use a random selection of 16 characters to change the shared key from time to time. Remember that you have to update all your applications, if you have any, to use the new shared key since they use it to generate the token. Don't use predicable text that can be compromised using brute force or guessed by a dictionary; use random characters so as to make the life of whoever is eavesdropping on you much harder. The **Edit Token Settings** form looks as follows:

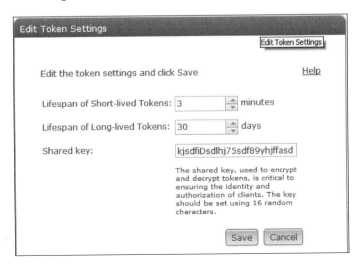

Web-tier – Web server security

ArcGIS token is an efficient authentication method; it comes built in with Server and provides you with basic security. However, it might not be the most effective security mechanism. In some instances, you will have security in place, you will have roles and users set up on an LDAP or Windows domain, and it will become hectic to repopulate those into ArcGIS for Server. That is why Server provides a channel to connect your Server site to the Windows domain where you can inherit all the configurations and let the Web server do the authentication every time someone requests a secured resource.

Enabling Web Security

To configure Web server security instead of tokens, access ArcGIS for Server Manager, click on **Security**, and edit **Configuration Settings** by clicking on the edit button. Choose the second option, **Users and roles from an existing enterprise system (LDAP or Windows Domain)**, and then click on **Next**.

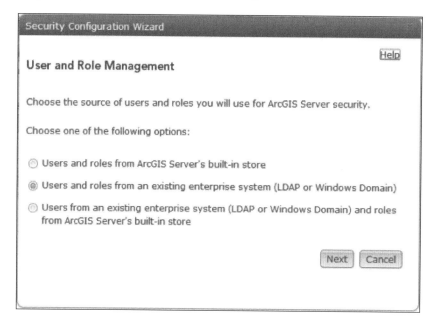

Server gives you the option to use an existing Windows domain or even configure your own LDAP server. For this exercise, we will use the Windows domain; make sure you have an active domain for this. Select **Windows Domain** and click on **Next** as shown in the following screenshot:

Next, you will have to enter a user that belongs to the domain; you want to pull this entire configuration from the domain, including users, permissions, and roles. It is important to note that this user must have basic permissions to read the domain information. Type the user credentials, click on **Test Connection** as shown in the following screenshot, and then click on **Next** if the test was successful.

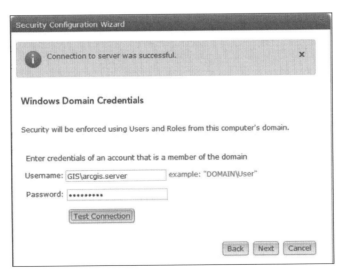

You will be prompted with an interesting choice: to use GIS server tier authentication or to use Web Tier authentication. GIS server tier is basically the token authentication; this will allow you to take advantage of the built-in token authentication while using your domain users instead of recreating your users and roles. The other option is Web Tier, which allows you to leave it for the Web server to do the authentication; in this case, IIS takes over and authenticates for you. Configuring Web Tier apparently requires you to do some configuration on the Web Adaptor, which makes sense as it is the link between your dedicated Web server and your GIS server. We will choose **Web Tier** for this exercise; click on **Next** as shown in the following screenshot and then click on **Finish** to save.

Configuring IIS

Note that the configuration settings have changed and users and roles are all pointing to the Windows domain; this will save huge administration tasks and will help centralize security. However, there is some work that needs to be done. First, the Web tier authentication requires a Web server, a dedicated one, which in turn requires a Web Adaptor to talk to. Therefore, before changing this security, you have to install the Web Adaptor. Return to *Chapter 1, Best Practices for Installing ArcGIS for Server*, for details regarding Web Adaptors. From your Windows Control Panel, open **Internet Information Services Manager**, expand the **Default Web Site** option, and select your Web Adaptor. Mine is **arcgis**; yours might be **wa** or **waadmin**. Then, double-click on **Authentication**, disable **Anonymous Authentication**, and enable **Windows Authentication** as shown in the following screenshot. This way, you force all authentications to come through Web server.

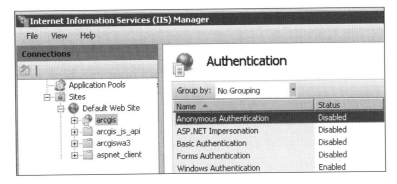

Adding new users and roles

You cannot use the role and user settings in ArcGIS for Server to modify roles; they have to be managed from the **Windows Domain Manager** window, where you will add roles and users to the domain. Use it to create the **View_Parcels** role.

Enabling security on GIS services

To enable security on the GIS services, click on the locked icon and assign the **GIS\View_Parcels** role to the **Parcels** GIS service as shown in the following screenshot. You have to make sure that the right users are assigned to this role or group in order to view them.

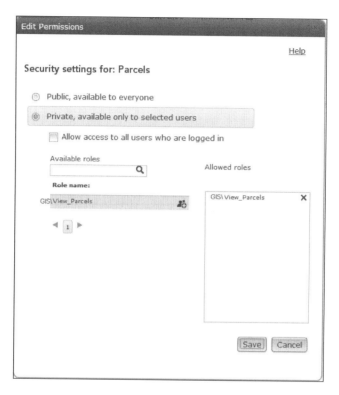

Connecting to a secured service

Using the same exercise in the *GIS server tier – ArcGIS token security* section, add a new role and assign it to your domain user. Then, log in to your machine using the domain user that has that role. You may use the same role name, **GIS\View_Parcels**. After following the same configuration, you will notice that the Web server doesn't even challenge the credentials; it just knows you from the Windows domain, which goes a long way towards saving time and efforts, and is much more secure and less annoying. Try accessing your Parcels web service from the Web using the URL `http://GIS-SERVER01/wa/rest/services/Parcels/MapServer`, for instance. Here, `wa` is the Web Adaptor you used. Domain users who are not authorized to view the Parcels web service will get the message **Error: User does not have permissions to access 'parcels.mapserver'**.

ArcGIS for Server Manager distilled

In versions 10.1 and 10.2, ArcGIS for Server has been completely rewritten to use pure web services in order to migrate to a potential Restful Service Oriented Architecture. Functionalities that have been written in the legacy **distributed component object model (DCOM)** back in ArcGIS Server 9.1 have been causing limitations and security issues, not to mention delays in the 64-bit architecture. When Esri moved away from DCOM, it allowed more flexibility to almost everything in Server, including Manager. You can now call any method in Server using an API, which really gave room to developers to do more and more with Server.

Creating users and roles

One of the best ways to control the ArcGIS for Server environment is to assign different users to each task. In the following exercise, we will create two user groups: Administrators, which will get the administrator role, and Authors, which will get the publisher role. This way, you can monitor everything based on the user credentials from the logs generated by Server. We will see this in *Chapter 8, Server Logs*.

 You can add also Reviewers group, which is a special user role that can view all services.

The various roles are as follows:

- **The administrator role**: Users assigned to this role can do anything the primary administrator account can, including creating and deleting users and roles, publishing services, deleting services, editing security parameters, and so on

- **The publisher role**: Users with a publisher role can delete and publish any service, but they cannot change security parameters in Manager

- **The user role**: This role can be assigned to a service so as to know who is allowed to use it

Testing access control

We will now create the following publishers and administrators for our Server site. From the **ArcGIS for Server Manager** window, log in to the site using the primary administrator account and go to **Security**.

Navigate to **Roles | New Role** and add the following role:

Name	Admins
Description	Site Administrators
Role Type	Administrator

Click on **New Role** and add the following role:

Name	Authors
Description	Service Authors
Role Type	Publisher

Navigate to **Users | New User** and add the following user:

Username	dave
Password	dave
Email	dave@agsa.com
Full name	Dave
Member of	Admins

Similarly, add the following users:

Username	kim	angel	anila
Password	kim	angel	anila
Email	kim@agsa.com	angel@agsa.com	anila@agsa.com
Full name	Kim	Angel	Anila
Member of	Admins	Authors	Authors

Your users list should look as the following screenshot shows after you finish:

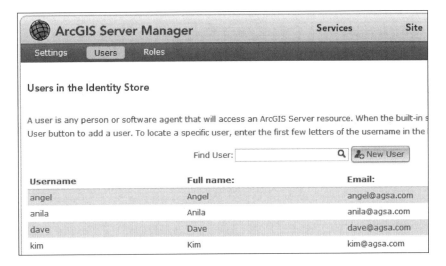

Go back to Manager, sign out of the primary administrator, and log in with dave instead. You will notice the exact same layout as shown in the following screenshot; you can still do pretty much whatever the primary admin can.

Go to **Security** and change the password for the primary administrator account, and then click on **Save** as shown in the following screenshot. Note that dave is a user with an administrator role and he can change the master super user.

Log out from the Manager and log in using the Anila credentials. Anila is an author, which means she is not supposed to change security settings, but she could stop and start services and even delete services. Note that you will see the following message when you log in. This means that some of the features are disabled.

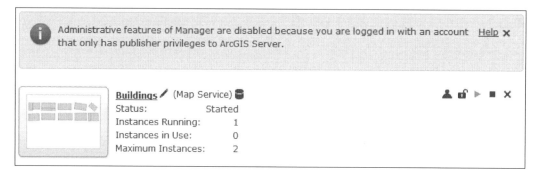

Try to click on **Security** and change the configuration settings; you will notice that it is grayed out, meaning that Anila does not have the privilege to change security settings in Manager.

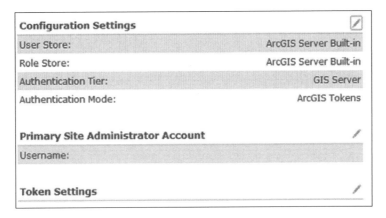

This is interesting because you now have control over users. One disadvantage, though, is that it is kind of unfair that publishers and administrators can have unrestricted control over services; any publisher or administrator can stop, delete, and start any service in the Site. This causes some control problems for those who want to tighten security. It would be great to add another layer of roles, where publishers can create new services but cannot delete services created by other publishers.

The administrator directory

The administrator directory is a backend, high-level access that grants you to do much more with your Server site. ArcGIS for Server Manager is an application developed on top of the administrator directory and is limited to whatever has been developed. There are many things you cannot do with the ArcGIS for Server Manager, such as deleting the Site or disabling the Primary Administration Account. You will be able to do that and much more using the Administrator API. To log in to the **Administrator Directory** form, type the following URL:

```
http://GIS-SERVER01:6080/arcgis/admin
```

You will get the following prompt. Log in with an administrator account; use `dave`.

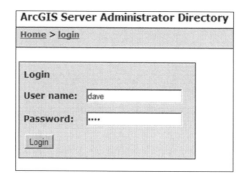

There are three main objects, which are as follows:

- **Resources**: This shows the available resources such as the **machines, clusters, services**, and so on

- **Supported Operations**: This shows the operations supported on these resources

- **Supported Interfaces**: This is **REST** most of the time since ArcGIS for Server is a RESTful system

Let us back up our Server site by exporting it to a file. From the **Supported Operations** list, click on **exportSite** and then click on **Export**. Note that this option is only available for Version 10.2 onwards.

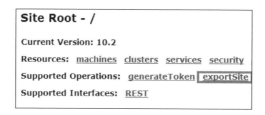

You will get a message with a link to download the exporting file, which will take you to a temporary location. Click on the link and then download the file.

You can use the admin directory to import the site back on a fresh installation and save a lot of time. Since this is all exposed to REST, you can write the code to access the Admin API and do monthly or weekly site backups in batch mode.

Disabling the primary administrator account

Your site now has three administrators—the two you created and the primary administrator. The primary administrator is a generic user; those with access to this account can do whatever they want, and it is hard to trace who did what as anybody from the system administrator team could have leaked these credentials. However, creating a dedicated account for individual users can create more control. This way, any action taken by an admin is recorded in the logfiles that we will discuss in the next chapter. This is why disabling the primary administrator account is a good practice. Perform the following steps to disable the primary administrator account:

1. Log in to the administrator directory using an administrator account, and from the site root resources, click on **Security**.

2. Click on **PSA**, which stands for **Primary System Administrator**.

3. From the supported operations, click on **Disable**.

Note that the status of the account is now disabled. To test if that worked, log out of the current session and log in using the primary system administrator account. You will see the following message, which prevents the primary administrator from accessing any resources:

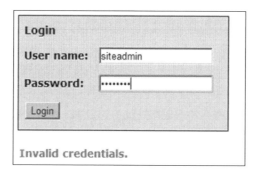

Hypertext Transfer Protocol Secure (HTTPS)

Whatever authentication method you have used to secure your GIS services, it will eventually achieve the one thing it is intended to, authentication. However, after authentication, the transmission of packets between client and server is all done in naked plain text. If you used tokens, someone can intercept and start working on breaking your token into its main components: the username and the password. If it is a long-lived token, chances are that it might be broken. Another eavesdropper might not even need to break the token; he/she will simply listen to the transmission, borrow the token, and re-use it in a **reply attack**. The same applies on the Web tier security, which is why securing the very channel on which the whole thing is staged is essential to protect all communication, and this is done using the HTTPS protocol.

A reply attack is a malicious network data transmission that seems valid. It is performed by repeating the request by changing a few of the transmission parameters for the attackers' advantage.

Summary

In this chapter, you have learned that ArcGIS for Server offers a good security mechanism to protect your GIS services, which are distributed across the network infrastructure. You now know that there are three methods to secure ArcGIS for Server. The first method, the GIS-tier, uses native ArcGIS token security, which does protection at the GIS service-level; the second one, the Web-tier, is the Web server security, which is applied at the Web server level; and the last one is the protocol security securing the transmission of the GIS data. The Web-tier security proves to be a better choice in an environment where security is crucial, while GIS-tier can be used for small-scale organizations. In the next chapter, you will learn how to analyze log messages generated by Server to find patterns that may help you optimize your environment.

8
Server Logs

Besides securing the GIS services, which we learned in the previous chapter, it is important to keep an eye on the services to verify that they are healthy and available for use. Monitoring a live system is crucial to maintaining stability and performance; not only to avoid potential failures but even for debugging and tracing back an event. That is why having a system record its activities results in a rich database of logs that can be used for investigation. Logfiles tell a fascinating story to those who can read it. They carry the history of all events narrated in thorough detail. ArcGIS for Server, like any other system, keeps logfiles for all events, from the basic "connection established" event to the severe "service failed to initiate" event. In this chapter, we will learn how to read logfiles and understand them in order to extract useful information that can help solving problems that might occur.

Logging levels

Recording events on Server is done at different levels. You can tell Server to log every single event as it happens or filter to record only fatal errors. Consequently, recording fine events generates more logs than recording only those messages with errors. There are seven logging levels, and these are described in the following Esri table:

Log level	Description
Severe	This level logs serious problems that require immediate attention. It only includes severe messages.
Warning	This level logs moderate problems that require attention. It also includes severe-level messages.
Info	This level logs common administrative messages from Server, including messages about service creation and startup. It also includes severe and warning messages.
Fine	This level logs common messages from users of Server, such as names of operation requests received. It includes severe, warning, and info messages.

Log level	Description
Verbose	This level logs messages providing more details about how Server completes an operation, such as whether each layer in a map service was drawn successfully, how fast the layer was drawn, and how long it took Server to access the layer's source data. This level includes severe, warning, info, and fine messages.
Debug	This level logs highly verbose messages designed for developers and support technicians who want to obtain a better understanding of the state of Server when troubleshooting. This level should not be used in a production environment as it may cause a significant decrease in Server performance.
Off	At this level, logging is turned off. Events are not logged with Server.

As you can see, Debug is the finest level and keeps Server busy with logging events, making other important tasks suffer.

Log analysis

Logs can be viewed and refreshed actively from the **ArcGIS for Server Manager** window as they are written. To see your current logfiles, go to **Manager** and activate the **Logs** tab:

Naturally, each GIS server generates its own logs and this is all saved by default at C:\arcgisserver\logs\. You cannot use a shared folder for this; each GIS server should generate its own logs in its directory, ArcGIS for Server aggregates those logs into the Server site, in a table view with filters options, which allows you to search through the logs. From the **View Log Messages** panel, click on **Query** to view the current logfiles as shown in the following screenshot. You might get messages different from mine.

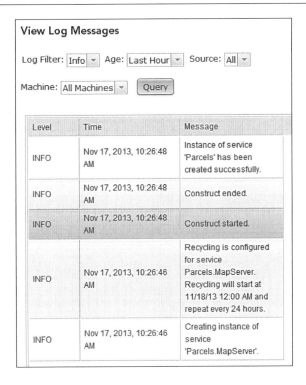

You might not have any messages if your current log level is set to only record errors, and there are no errors. To change the log level, click on **Settings**. From the **Log Settings** form, select **Verbose** from the **Log Level** drop-down list. You can set the logs to be cleared automatically if you want to. Keep the rest of the settings intact and click on the **Save** button.

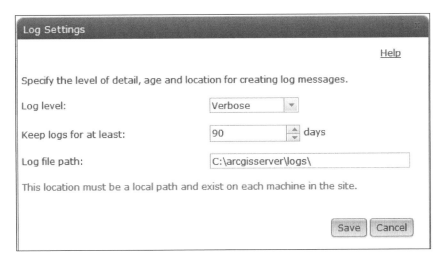

By default, the logs are kept on the GIS server for three months. If you are planning to keep the logs for longer than that, perhaps for offline analysis, you may want to archive them periodically and delete them. Generally, clearing the logs is better for performance. This will be discussed in the coming pages.

> **Best practice**
> Since logs are saved to disk frequently, they use high IO. It is recommended that you point the log path to a local directory, preferably on a **Solid State Drive (SSD)** for best performance.

Now, let us see how the logs are being generated. First of all, let us clear all the logs to start afresh. To do that, click on **Delete Logs** from **ArcGIS for Server Manager** and then click on **Yes**, as shown in the following screenshot:

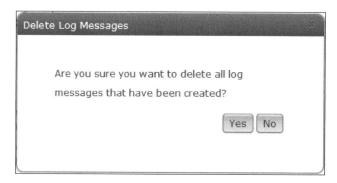

Now that the logs are cleared, we will activate the `parcels` service by simply visiting the **REST URL** and then checking the log. You must remember how we get the REST URL from a service; we explained that in *Chapter 3, Consuming GIS Services*. The following is the REST URL:

`http://GIS-SERVER01:6080/arcgis/rest/services/Parcels/MapServer`

Type the REST URL on a new browser page and press *Enter*. You should see something like the following screenshot if you have access to the service:

Go back to your logs and click on **Query** to refresh the page. You should see one message in the table. You might see other messages from Server that happened to be executed at that particular time but look for this one:

Level	Time	Message	Source	Machine	User Name
INFO	Nov 17, 2013, 11:18:26 AM	Request user: Anonymous user, Service: Parcels/ MapServer	Rest	GIS-SERVER01	Anonymous user

The level is **INFO**, which means a detailed event; it says a request user from REST consumed the Parcels Map Service and `GIS-SERVER01` served that request. If you have security enabled, you would even know which user consumed that service. Now, let us take it to the next level. On the **Parcels REST** page, click on **ArcGIS JavaScript** to view the map with the service loaded.

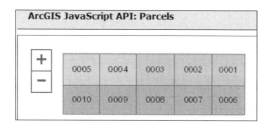

Go back to the log view and click on **Query** to refresh; make sure the **Log Filter** dropdown is set to **Verbose**. A fleet of messages was generated from our last action; we will take a look at each line and analyze it.

 There are many columns that can be displayed on the log table and you can show or hide them from the **Columns** button.

For a better view, you can click on the **Printer Friendly View** link, which will display a text format version of this table in a new page.

This is the log we are going to analyze; we will start from the first line:

```
INFO, Nov 17, 2013, 11:29:17 AM, Request user: Anonymous user,
    Service: Parcels/MapServer Rest.
```

This is a request to consume the service. You can use this identifier to measure how many times a service has been requested.

```
FINE Nov 17, 2013, 11:29:17 AM REST request received. Request size
    is 178 characters. Parcels.MapServer
```

The preceding line is appended if there is more work to be followed; it shows the request size in bytes.

```
FINE Nov 17, 2013, 11:29:17 AM Begin ExportMapImage
    Parcels.MapServer
```

The process is so fast that we are still in the same second. The preceding line of code tells us that the **Export Map Image** process just started. This is the big process where Server exports an image of the desired area; however, there is still more work to follow to create the actual image. You can start measuring the drawing time of a certain service from this line.

```
VERBOSE Nov 17, 2013, 11:29:17 AM Begining of preparation.
    Parcels.MapServer
VERBOSE Nov 17, 2013, 11:29:17 AM End of preparation.
    Parcels.MapServer
```

The preceding two lines highlight the preparation of the export image process. They usually happen very fast.

```
FINE Nov 17, 2013, 11:29:17 AM
    Extent:1467314.863829,2191233.084700,2574598.328396,2702665.79038;
        Size:1574,727; Scale:2658831.00Parcels.MapServer
```

A map needs an initial extent coordinates for it to draw. At the first call of the service, Server implicitly sends the default full extent to draw the map. After that, the user will explicitly request a new extent, each time he/she zooms in or pans the map.

```
VERBOSE Nov 17, 2013, 11:29:17 AM Beginning of layer draw: Parcels
    Parcels.MapServer
```

Since we only have one layer, you will see one occurrence of this line; however, you will see these lines reappear with more layers and there will be more logs to follow.

```
VERBOSE Nov 17, 2013, 11:29:17 AM Execute Query Parcels.MapServer
```

I consider this one of the most important lines; this is where the database is advised and queried to get the actual features. You can make a good measurement here by monitoring how long an execute query takes. If this takes a long time to execute, you might want to consult your DBA to look into tuning the database.

```
VERBOSE Nov 17, 2013, 11:29:17 AM Symbol Drawing Parcels.MapServer
VERBOSE Nov 17, 2013, 11:29:17 AM Data Access Parcels.MapServer
VERBOSE Nov 17, 2013, 11:29:17 AM Symbolizing Parcels.MapServer
```

Symbology work, depending on the user, can be executed either on the server or on the client. Since we are running on a browser, the symbology drawing will be carried on the client's browser by JavaScript. Note that this is only the symbology drawing; the labeling is done in another step.

```
VERBOSE Nov 17, 2013, 11:29:17 AM Number of features drawn: 10
   Parcels.MapServer
```

This message shows the number of features that have been drawn. This line is useful if you want to know how many features are retrieved for each request and monitor the performance.

```
VERBOSE Nov 17, 2013, 11:29:17 AM End of layer draw: Parcels
   Parcels.MapServer
```

This line signifies the end of layer drawing; you should now start seeing the map, but with no labels.

```
VERBOSE Nov 17, 2013, 11:29:17 AM Beginning of labeling phase
   (labeling and label draw) Parcels.MapServer
```

Now that the symbology work is done, the labeling will start. This will give you even more measurement indicators for performance.

```
VERBOSE Nov 17, 2013, 11:29:17 AM Symbol Drawing Parcels.MapServer
```

It draws the font symbol as described in the layer description which can be found in the layer properties.

```
VERBOSE Nov 17, 2013, 11:29:17 AM Number of features drawn: 10
   Parcels.MapServer
```

The preceding line indicates that the features have been labeled successfully.

```
VERBOSE Nov 17, 2013, 11:29:17 AM End of labeling phase (labeling
   and label draw) Parcels.MapServer
```

The preceding line marks the end of the labeling phase.

```
FINE Nov 17, 2013, 11:29:17 AM End ExportMapImage
  Parcels.MapServer
```

The map image has been exported successfully; we will attempt to deliver it to the client after this.

```
FINE Nov 17, 2013, 11:29:17 AM REST request successfully
  processed. Response size is 6364 characters. Parcels.MapServer
```

The last message describes the response map, which is a 6K map image. My Server is so fast that the whole thing happened in the same second. This is not much by way of a log analysis. However, in the next topic we will attempt to analyze a much richer log and will try to answer some questions.

Exercise – finding the bottleneck

A client is suffering from severe performance with their new GIS web application. The client has provided you with a detailed verbose log of the default extent, hoping you will find what is wrong with the application. There are three services: Pole, Powercable, and ServicePoint. The application points to the three services and displays them using JavaScript API. You can find the logfile in the support files under 7364EN_08_Files\AGSA\Log.

The logfile

The following logs were generated on Nov 17, 2013 between 11:31:00 and 11:31:59. They were generated during the last minute of the request duration.

```
FINE Nov 17, 2013, 11:31:29 AM REST request successfully
  processed. Response size is 10976 characters.
    PowerCable.MapServer
FINE Nov 17, 2013, 11:31:29 AM End ExportMapImage
  PowerCable.MapServer
VERBOSE Nov 17, 2013, 11:31:29 AM End of labeling phase (labeling
  and label draw) PowerCable.MapServer
VERBOSE Nov 17, 2013, 11:31:19 AM Number of features drawn: 35
  PowerCable.MapServer
VERBOSE Nov 17, 2013, 11:31:19 AM Symbol Drawing
  PowerCable.MapServer
VERBOSE Nov 17, 2013, 11:31:19 AM Beginning of labeling phase
  (labeling and label draw) PowerCable.MapServer
VERBOSE Nov 17, 2013, 11:31:19 AM End of layer draw: PowerCable
  PowerCable.MapServer
```

VERBOSE Nov 17, 2013, 11:31:19 AM Number of features drawn: 35
  PowerCable.MapServer

VERBOSE Nov 17, 2013, 11:31:19 AM Symbol Drawing
  PowerCable.MapServer

VERBOSE Nov 17, 2013, 11:31:19 AM Data Access PowerCable.MapServer

VERBOSE Nov 17, 2013, 11:31:19 AM Symbolizing PowerCable.MapServer

VERBOSE Nov 17, 2013, 11:31:19 AM Execute Query
  PowerCable.MapServer

VERBOSE Nov 17, 2013, 11:31:19 AM Beginning of layer draw:
  PowerCable PowerCable.MapServer

FINE Nov 17, 2013, 11:31:19 AM
  Extent:1467314.863829,2191233.084700,2574598.328396,2702665.79038;
    Size:1574,727; Scale:2658831.00PowerCable.MapServer

VERBOSE Nov 17, 2013, 11:31:19 AM End of preparation.
  PowerCable.MapServer

VERBOSE Nov 17, 2013, 11:31:19 AM Begining of preparation.
  PowerCable.MapServer

FINE Nov 17, 2013, 11:31:19 AM Begin ExportMapImage
  PowerCable.MapServer

FINE Nov 17, 2013, 11:31:19 AM REST request received. Request size
  is 178 characters. PowerCable.MapServer

INFO Nov 17, 2013, 11:31:19 AM Request user: Anonymous user,
  Service: PowerCable/MapServer Rest

FINE Nov 17, 2013, 11:31:19 AM REST request successfully
  processed. Response size is 5764 characters.
    ServicePoint.MapServer

FINE Nov 17, 2013, 11:31:19 AM End ExportMapImage
  ServicePoint.MapServer

VERBOSE Nov 17, 2013, 11:31:15 AM End of labeling phase (labeling
  and label draw) ServicePoint.MapServer

VERBOSE Nov 17, 2013, 11:31:15 AM Number of features drawn: 10
  ServicePoint.MapServer

VERBOSE Nov 17, 2013, 11:31:15 AM Symbol Drawing
  ServicePoint.MapServer

VERBOSE Nov 17, 2013, 11:31:15 AM Beginning of labeling phase
  (labeling and label draw) ServicePoint.MapServer

VERBOSE Nov 17, 2013, 11:31:15 AM End of layer draw: ServicePoint
  ServicePoint.MapServer

VERBOSE Nov 17, 2013, 11:31:15 AM Number of features drawn: 10
  ServicePoint.MapServer

VERBOSE Nov 17, 2013, 11:31:01 AM Symbol Drawing
  ServicePoint.MapServer

VERBOSE Nov 17, 2013, 11:31:01 AM Data Access
  ServicePoint.MapServer

VERBOSE Nov 17, 2013, 11:31:01 AM Symbolizing
  ServicePoint.MapServer

```
VERBOSE Nov 17, 2013, 11:31:01 AM Execute Query
    ServicePoint.MapServer
VERBOSE Nov 17, 2013, 11:31:01 AM Beginning of layer draw:
    ServicePoint ServicePoint.MapServer
FINE Nov 17, 2013, 11:31:01 AM
    Extent:1467314.863829,2191233.084700,2574598.328396,2702665.79038;
      Size:1574,727; Scale:2658831.00ServicePoint.MapServer
VERBOSE Nov 17, 2013, 11:31:01 AM End of preparation.
    ServicePoint.MapServer
VERBOSE Nov 17, 2013, 11:31:01 AM Begining of preparation.
    ServicePoint.MapServer
FINE Nov 17, 2013, 11:31:01 AM Begin ExportMapImage
    ServicePoint.MapServer
FINE Nov 17, 2013, 11:31:01 AM REST request received. Request size
    is 993 characters. ServicePoint.MapServer
INFO Nov 17, 2013, 11:31:01 AM Request user: Anonymous user,
    Service: ServicePoint/MapServer Rest
FINE Nov 17, 2013, 11:31:01 AM REST request successfully
    processed. Response size is 96478 characters. Pole.MapServer
FINE Nov 17, 2013, 11:31:01 AM End ExportMapImage Pole.MapServer
VERBOSE Nov 17, 2013, 11:31:01 AM End of labeling phase (labeling
    and label draw) Pole.MapServer
VERBOSE Nov 17, 2013, 11:31:01 AM Number of features drawn: 6241
    Pole.MapServer
```

The following logs were generated between 11:29:00 and 11:29:45. They were generated during the first minute of the request duration.

```
VERBOSE Nov 17, 2013, 11:29:45 AM Symbol Drawing Pole.MapServer
VERBOSE Nov 17, 2013, 11:29:45 AM Beginning of labeling phase
    (labeling and label draw) Pole.MapServer
VERBOSE Nov 17, 2013, 11:29:45 AM End of layer draw: Pole
    Pole.MapServer
VERBOSE Nov 17, 2013, 11:29:45 AM Number of features drawn: 6241
    Pole.MapServer
VERBOSE Nov 17, 2013, 11:29:17 AM Symbol Drawing Pole.MapServer
VERBOSE Nov 17, 2013, 11:29:17 AM Data Access Pole.MapServer
VERBOSE Nov 17, 2013, 11:29:17 AM Symbolizing Pole.MapServer
VERBOSE Nov 17, 2013, 11:29:01 AM Execute Query Pole.MapServer
VERBOSE Nov 17, 2013, 11:29:00 AM Beginning of layer draw: Pole
    Pole.MapServer
FINE Nov 17, 2013, 11:29:00 AM
    Extent:1467314.863829,2191233.084700,2574598.328396,2702665.79038;
      Size:1574,727; Scale:2658831.00Pole.MapServer
VERBOSE Nov 17, 2013, 11:29:00 AM End of preparation.
    Pole.MapServer
```

```
VERBOSE Nov 17, 2013, 11:29:00 AM Begining of preparation.
  Pole.MapServer
FINE Nov 17, 2013, 11:29:00 AM Begin ExportMapImage Pole.MapServer
FINE Nov 17, 2013, 11:29:00 AM REST request received. Request size
  is 214 characters. Pole.MapServer
INFO Nov 17, 2013, 11:29:00 AM Request user: Anonymous user,
  Service: Pole/MapServer Rest
```

Analysis and findings

Let us start at the beginning, reading the logs from bottom to top; you will find that the first service to be requested is the `Pole` service at 11:29:00.

```
INFO Nov 17, 2013, 11:29:00 AM Request user: Anonymous user,
  Service: Pole/MapServer Rest
```

If you follow the log timeline, you will notice that the time stamp remains relatively the same up until the execution of the query, which takes a good 16 seconds to execute. A query that takes this long could mean one of two things: it is a complex query that takes a lot of time to parse and execute by the DBMS, or it is a simple query but returns a large set of results. Following are the two lines which marked the elapsed query:

```
VERBOSE Nov 17, 2013, 11:29:17 AM Symbolizing Pole.MapServer
VERBOSE Nov 17, 2013, 11:29:01 AM Execute Query Pole.MapServer
```

The query returns more than 6000 features. This is not normal for a simple request as 6000 features takes around half a minute to draw with symbology; plus, labeling this large set of features takes more than a minute.

```
VERBOSE Nov 17, 2013, 11:29:45 AM Number of features drawn: 6241
  Pole.MapServer
```

We managed to find the first bottleneck, and we now need to identify what caused it. The first thing we will investigate is the scale range of the pole layer. When we check the source document used to publish this service, we might find that this layer is set to draw at all scales. This is a problem because viewing the pole layer at a higher scale caused fetching the 6000 features, resulting in a performance penalty of 16 seconds. Look at the following screenshot, which describes how the pole layer is set to draw at all scales:

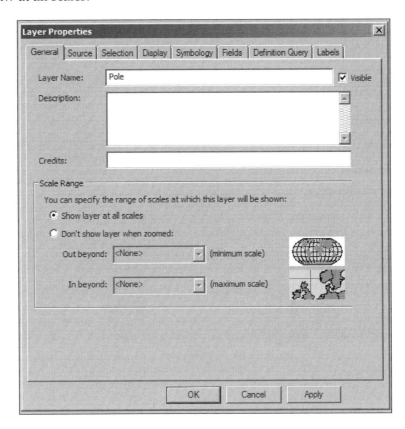

To solve this problem, we need to set a good scale for the pole layer. This should save around two minutes of both executing and drawing time. To set a scale for the pole layer, open **Layer Properties** in ArcMap. Then, select **Don't Show layer when zoomed** from the **Scale Range** box. Type 1500 in the **Out beyond** textbox, which makes this layer invisible beyond that scale.

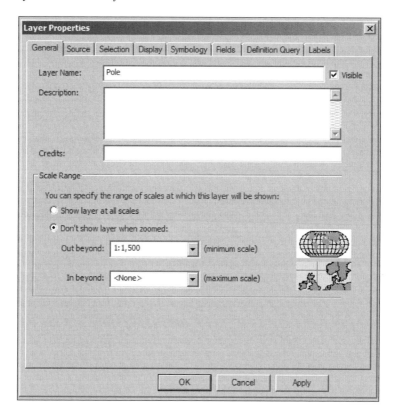

If we continue reading the log, we will notice that the ServicePoint service doesn't take time to execute. However, it does take 14 seconds to draw only 10 features, which means that the symbology used for this layer is a complex one:

```
VERBOSE Nov 17, 2013, 11:31:15 AM Number of features drawn: 10
   ServicePoint.MapServer
VERBOSE Nov 17, 2013, 11:31:01 AM Symbol Drawing
   ServicePoint.MapServer
```

The following is an example of a complex symbology:

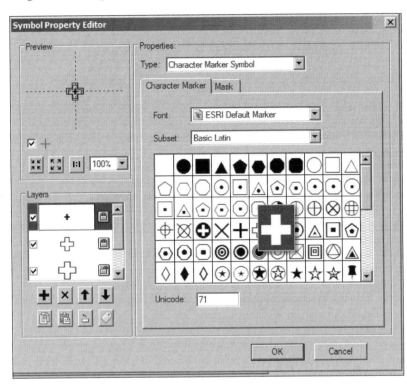

To fix this issue, we must use a much simpler symbology. Avoid using complex or multilayered symbols as they draw much slower. Use hollow symbols instead of filled or patterned ones. Hollow symbols do not need to be painted on the inside and significantly improve performance for larger sets of data. Also avoid using transparency in the symbols; this takes a lot of memory and graphics power to draw, thus slowing you down. If you have to use complex symbology, make sure to set a lower scale to the layer so you fetch fewer features. I have compiled the following diagram for general guidelines on the use of symbology:

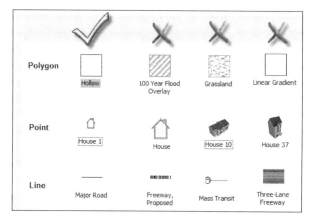

Finally, we find that the `PowerCable` layer does execute and draw comfortably. However, it takes 10 seconds just to label a few features, and this means the labeling used for this layer is complex. This might be because of a special script labeling used to draw the labels concatenating multiple fields and values:

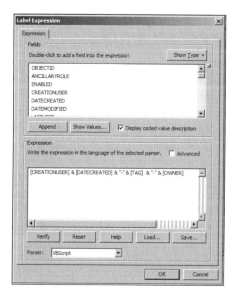

The simplest way to solve this is to use simple labeling or remove labeling all together. If labeling is essential on this layer, you might want to consider converting the layer to the annotation layer. This Esri resource describes how this can be done: `http://bit.ly/1jvRIMx`.

You have managed to identify and solve three problems that could potentially save three minutes of response time for the application, and this is all thanks to your skills at reading the logs.

Clearing Server logs

Clearing logs files is an important step that you need to carry out frequently on your Server. As logs pile up, Server struggles to update it. For instance, updating a 10-byte file is not like updating a 10-megabyte file. It takes I/O and latency, which affects the overall performance, especially if you are running on a fine level log. Here is how to clean the logs: from the **ArcGIS for Server Manager** window, activate the **Logs** tab and click on **Delete Logs** to clear all the logs from all GIS servers. You can also use the settings to set an expiry for the logs. However, it is recommended that you use severe mode in a production environment unless you are monitoring the system.

Summary

Server logs are a double-edged sword. You can use them to monitor your system effectively, but they can cause performance penalties if they pile up. In this chapter, you have learned the different levels of Server logs and how and which level you should configure your Server setup to. You also learned how to analyze the logs and extract useful information to optimize your services and detect a malfunction in one of your Server components, if any. In the coming appendix, you will learn some rules of thumb for selecting the right hardware for your ArcGIS for Server setup.

Selecting the Right Hardware

Hardware is the set of cogs that makes the system operate. If a company wants to deploy software, it will require hardware to deploy it on. Purchasing expensive servers with highest specifications can be the choice for most companies in this case. However, knowing the software and hardware requirements and the estimated usage can help the company make smart decisions, save a lot of money, and have a system that runs efficiently and effectively. If you have a maximum of 500 users combined, it is costly and inefficient to purchase hardware that can serve 5,000 users. This section is dedicated to guide you to pick the hardware you need and distribute it carefully so that ArcGIS for Server can comfortably serve your maximum users.

Licensing – more machines or more power

The best way to select hardware is to understand the software you are going to use it for. ArcGIS for Server is licensed and based on processer cores, not users; this means the more cores you have, the more expensive the product becomes. For example, let us say you want to purchase a four-core license. This can give you many hardware solution options: you can get one server with quad-core CPU, or you can get two dual-core servers. If you could even find a single-core server these days, you can get four of those. But the question is which one of those solutions is suitable? According to Moore's law, computer power doubles every 18 months; this can be applied to the price as well, where the cost of the hardware drops. Although this depends on other factors including the clock speed of the core itself, having four single-core servers can theoretically give the same power as a one quad-core server given that they have relatively the same frequency. There is one thing which is important to be noted: not all the ArcGIS for Server tasks run on parallel processing. This means if you have four tasks or requests to be executed, it is more efficient to line them up on four moderately strong servers rather than stacking them up on one powerful server.

Four physical servers have their own dedicated memory and bus routes linked in a high-speed cluster, which gives more availability than one quad-core server and it is definitely cheaper. This way you can save a lot for the same or even more power; the key is not to be tricked by gimmicks of the hardware marketers and to know your requirements before purchasing the hardware. Esri has a dedicated website that compares different hardware and provides recommendations for the best hardware for Server; you can take a look at it at `http://www.esri.com/systemdesign`.

Choosing the number of cores

The number of cores defines the licensing for ArcGIS for Server and eventually how many users you are going to serve. According to Esri, a CPU in a GIS server under average conditions can support about four concurrently active service instances. The key is that if you are planning to serve users, not all will be sending requests at the same time; this means we can safely load more than four users on a single core. This also means a quad-core processor can serve up to 16 concurrent users. Let's do the math: assume an average GIS request takes about 200ms to execute and a single core can serve up to four requests in parallel, which means it can execute all the four requests in just 200ms. How much time does this core take to serve 1,000 requests assuming that they all came in at the same time? The answer is simple. We divide the requests by four and then multiply them by 200ms, which is the time required to execute each request in parallel. It takes 50 seconds to execute 1,000 GIS requests, four at a time, until they are all exhausted. Adding another core will shave half of that time off and serve as many requests. You can use the following formula to calculate the time required:

$$T = \frac{QX}{4C}$$

Where:

Variable	Description
T	Time required to execute Q in seconds
C	The number of cores in a processor
Q	Maximum number of requests or users
X	The average execution time for a request, usually 0.2 seconds

As seen in the previous table, T is the total execution time in seconds to complete Q number of requests; this can also signify the waiting time in the service. As per the equation, adding more cores (C) will decrease T, and having more clock speed will decrease X and will potentially bring T down. Similarly, you can reverse the equation to determine the number of cores required to serve, for example, 2,000 requests in 30 seconds as follows:

$$C = \frac{QX}{4T}$$

We substitute T with 30 seconds; this is my threshold, X will be 0.2 seconds, Q is 2,000, which leads to 3.3 cores, since there is no processor with as many number of cores. The nearest thing is a quad-core processor.

$$C = \frac{2000(0.2)}{4(30)} = 4 \; Cores$$

Choosing the size of memory

ArcGIS for Server requires a 64 instruction-set CPU in order to run. Your Server can run effectively on a quad-core 64-bit processor with minimum 8 GB RAM Server. Although, as your services and users increase, your 8 GB RAM will be drained quickly. The good thing about memory is that adding more is always better, since memory is cheap and you are not licensed for memory, at least not for ArcGIS for Server. Theoretically, a 16 GB RAM GIS server can serve up to 100 users if you were planning to have five services on one GIS server. You can replace that GIS server with two 8 GB RAMs as well. I have developed another rule of thumb to determine how much memory you require for each GIS server.

$$R = \frac{S.U}{20G \; \sqrt{3}}$$

Where:

Variable	Description
R	RAM in Gigabytes per GIS server
S	Maximum number of services anticipated
U	Maximum number of users expected (non-concurrent)
G	Number of GIS servers on the Site

As seen in the previous table, R is the minimum amount of memory in a single GIS server required to make an optimal setup. It is measured in Gigabytes. You may round this number to the next nearest market-available RAM. For instance, if you got 13 GB, you may round it 16 GB. S is the total number of web services you are planning to have; this includes services that you are using; services that are not used should not be included in this equation. U is the maximum number of users you expect; note that this is the user and not requests. G is the number of GIS servers that will split the load. If you wish to have less RAM, you should increase this variable as these two variables are indirectly proportional. Let us say you want to serve 200 users and you anticipate publishing maybe 20 services running on 2 GIS servers. Using the preceding formula, you will get the size of memory you need as shown:

$$R = \frac{20(200)}{20(2)\sqrt{3}} = 58GB$$

Although this seems like a lot of memory to have for each GIS server, it is the maximum you need for the worst-case scenario. It is definitely a figure that can help decide the size of memory needed. Serving 200 users that may consume all 20 services of course will spawn a lot of processes, and having 64 GB of memory will be enough to serve those requests and other applications that are running on the GIS servers including the database clients. If you increased the number of Servers (G) to 4, you will only need 32 GB per server. This will help you make smart decisions based on quotations you will be getting from hardware vendors.

Summary

This appendix has described how to select the right hardware for your ArcGIS for Server environment by providing some rules of thumb. By calculating the number of cores and memory required to serve your users, you can now estimate the level of hardware you need to efficiently set up Server on a good hardware that can run comfortably and serve your users without experiencing any deficiencies or requiring upgrading frequently. The next appendix will explain the history of architectures of ArcGIS for Server 10.1 and 10.2 versus the prior versions 10 and 9.x.

B
Server Architecture

During its lifetime, ArcGIS for Server has proven resilient to the advances of technologies. It managed to adopt and evolve as more users started migrating to the technology despite the limitations of its architecture at that time. With 10.1, Esri has introduced a completely new architecture. This enabled the product to consume resources more efficiently and increase the execution throughput effectively utilizing the 64-bit instruction set and hyper multithreading. Upgrading from the previous architecture didn't come free of pain to Server users. The users, especially the developers, had to rewrite their websites along with any libraries they developed if they wanted to migrate to the new version. In this appendix, we will explain the difference between the previous and the new architectures, emphasizing on the benefits of the new architecture.

The rise of ArcGIS Server

When Esri released ArcIMS back in 2000, which was solely designed with one purpose in mind, to share maps over the Internet, they never anticipated that it would take off. The web was at its boom, but people were still reluctant to move from their comfort desktop zone to web browsers. Smart phones hadn't tipped yet, so there was no need for mobility and portability with the GIS data. Despite all that, ArcIMS did spread, and it became one of the most used software for sharing maps. The problem with ArcIMS was that it wasn't designed to run on a distributed environment. Changing the architecture of the product was indeed expensive, especially with all these users having stabled their customizations around this technology. The President of Esri has always been fascinated with the concept of cloud computing and sharing maps over thin clients. Therefore, Esri decided to start a new project. The project was named ArcGIS Server.

ArcGIS Server was designed to scale on multiple machines and was equipped with a load-balancing module to balance the requests between the different machines. Not only you could author, publish, and share maps on Server, but it was also equipped with a new feature, geoprocessing, which made it replace ArcIMS altogether. Users can now run tasks on their data to be processed and returned, and they can even combine different tasks into models and create more complex geoprocessing models. Recently, Esri changed the name of ArcGIS Server to ArcGIS for Server for marketing purposes. Ten years after its release, Esri ceases the support of ArcIMS and refocuses its resources on ArcGIS for Server.

Server architecture 9.x-10.0

The success of ArcGIS for Desktop and the rich fine-grained library of ArcObjects have helped shaping ArcGIS for Server. Server was designed around DCOM technology, which is the core of ArcGIS for Desktop. Although that decision made it possible to ship ArcGIS for Server swiftly, it did introduce a few problems and limitations along the way.

SOM and SOC

Prior to 10.1, GIS services had a number of instances hosted by a set of processes. These processes are called the **Server Object Container** (**SOC**) because as their name indicates, they act as a container for the instances. The SOC can be configured to run on separate machines to utilize more resources. These SOC processes are managed by another process called **Server Object Manager** (**SOM**). The SOM process can be hosted in a separate machine or in the same machine the SOC is hosted. All the requests are forwarded to the SOM process to control the requests' distribution and load balancing. All communications between SOM and SOC machines are bounded by DCOM, which requires special ports to be opened in order for the data exchange to be successful.

Web server

The Web server is another component of ArcGIS Server that can be installed separately. Websites are published on the Web server, which in turn connects to the SOM machine to consume services.

DCOM

DCOM is a classic Windows approach, which uses dynamic-link libraries for communication. All connections between SOM and SOCs are done through DCOM. There is a built-in Web server as we discussed in *Chapter 1, Best Practices for Installing ArcGIS for Server*, which replaced all the DCOM internal communication, thus avoiding opening all RPC ports that require firewall permissions. The communication in the new ArcGIS for Server is all wrapped using REST. SOAP is still used in the data exchange between ArcGIS for Desktop and Server. Please refer to *Chapter 2, Authoring Web Services*, for more details on this subject. The following diagram shows the ArcGIS Server system architecture:

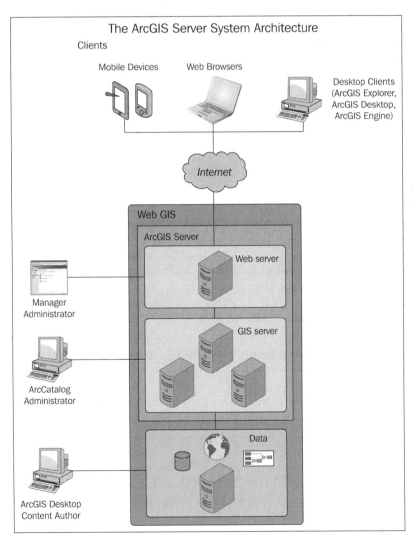

Benefits of a 64-bit architecture

By replacing DCOM, Server has decoupled itself from the ArcGIS for Desktop environment, making it less dependent on the C++ library and the fine-grained ArcObjects, which were written and compiled on a 32-bit architecture. Esri designed a new architecture for Server that allowed migration to the 64-bit architecture, completely rewriting the code for Server along the way. I always like to use this metaphor when explaining the benefits of a 64-bit architecture. Imagine an eight-lane highway where four lanes are used for trucks while regular cars can use the full eight-lane highway. Cars will be able to navigate more smoothly on the highway unlike the trucks, which have only four lanes also shared by other cars. The following figure describes briefly the difference between 64-bit and 32-bit systems in a CPU. Notice how the 64-bit bus is wider, which allows more bits to flow between the memory and the CPU.

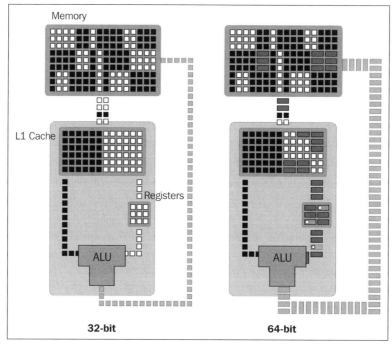

[Photo Credit to http://arstechnica.com/]

Trucks are the 32-bit applications running on a 64-bit processor, while regular cars are the 64-bit application getting the full advantage of the 64-bit architecture. The 64-bit applications will get more throughputs in terms of processed bytes and can address more than 4 GB of memory. This is practically useful for raster and image processing where huge chunks of data are moved to the memory where it is sliced and diced.

The CPUs have small storage units called registers. Although registers are very fast in storage and retrieval, they can store a small amount of data. In 32-bit CPUs there are generally eight 32-bit registers. Each register can store up to 4 bytes for fast CPU processing. If all registers are used, the CPU uses the RAM to store and process the data. This process takes more time of course, since the CPU has to send a request to access the RAM and wait for a signal back. In a 64-bit architecture, the size of the registers has been increased to 64-bit (8 bytes). This allows more room in the CPU to store and process more bits before it uses the RAM. Look at the following figure for clarification:

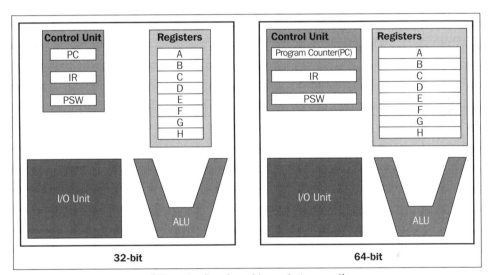

[Photo Credit to http://arstechnica.com/]

Summary

In this appendix, you have learned the difference between the old and the new ArcGIS for Server architecture. You now know the timeline of the hardware and software enhancement that Esri has implemented during its journey of ArcGIS for Server. Server has survived the 32-bit architecture locking-trap, which ArcGIS for Desktop still suffers from and jumped into the more effective 64-bit architecture. Reworking ArcGIS for Server to utilize the 64-bit architecture has improved the software performance to a completely new level.

Index

G

geodatabase
  about 10, 11
  enabling 121-126
  map, authoring with 52-57
Geographical Rich Site Summary. *See* GeoRSS
Geographic Markup Language (GML) 43
geoprocessing service
  about 69
  mapping 160, 161
geoprocessing tools 146
GeoRSS 73
GIS-REMOTE01 151
GIS server installation
  about 25
  Master GIS server installation 25
  Secondary GIS server installation 28
GIS servers 7, 10, 107
GIS server tier
  about 167, 168
  ArcGIS token security, enabling 169, 170
  connecting, to secured service 174-176
  roles, adding 170, 171
  security, enabling on GIS services 172, 173
  shared key security 177
  users, adding 170
GIS service instance 131
GIS services
  about 39, 49
  authoring 127-129
  database design 112
  database indexing, used for optimization 116
  deploying 121
  designing 112
  entity-relationship (ER) diagram 113-116
  mapping, to clusters 157
  map services 49
  nominating 111
  OGC services 66
  planning 110
  requirements, analyzing 110
  security, enabling on 172, 173
  testing 69-72

using, for analysis 101
using, for editing 94
using, for visualization 77
GIS services design
  about 117
  multiple map services 120
  single map service 117, 118
GIS services, using for analysis
  outage cause, finding 101-107
  prerequisites 101
GIS software
  services, consuming from 77
gliffy
  about 113
  URL 113
Google Earth 48
  about 84
  using 85, 86
Google Geocoder 48

H

Hadoop 161
Hadoop architecture 160
hardware
  about 211
  selecting 211
hardware requisites, Testing Installation Track 15
high-affinity map service
  mapping 159
high isolation configuration, process 137, 138
HTTP 10
Hypertext Transfer Protocol Secure (HTTPS) 190

I

IIS
  ASP, enabling on 40
  configuring 181
indexing 116
info log level 193
installation tracks
  about 7

Thank you for buying
Administering ArcGIS for Server

About Packt Publishing

Packt, pronounced 'packed', published its first book "Mastering phpMyAdmin for Effective MySQL Management" in April 2004 and subsequently continued to specialize in publishing highly focused books on specific technologies and solutions.

Our books and publications share the experiences of your fellow IT professionals in adapting and customizing today's systems, applications, and frameworks. Our solution based books give you the knowledge and power to customize the software and technologies you're using to get the job done. Packt books are more specific and less general than the IT books you have seen in the past. Our unique business model allows us to bring you more focused information, giving you more of what you need to know, and less of what you don't.

Packt is a modern, yet unique publishing company, which focuses on producing quality, cutting-edge books for communities of developers, administrators, and newbies alike. For more information, please visit our website: www.packtpub.com.

About Packt Enterprise

In 2010, Packt launched two new brands, Packt Enterprise and Packt Open Source, in order to continue its focus on specialization. This book is part of the Packt Enterprise brand, home to books published on enterprise software – software created by major vendors, including (but not limited to) IBM, Microsoft and Oracle, often for use in other corporations. Its titles will offer information relevant to a range of users of this software, including administrators, developers, architects, and end users.

Writing for Packt

We welcome all inquiries from people who are interested in authoring. Book proposals should be sent to author@packtpub.com. If your book idea is still at an early stage and you would like to discuss it first before writing a formal book proposal, contact us; one of our commissioning editors will get in touch with you.

We're not just looking for published authors; if you have strong technical skills but no writing experience, our experienced editors can help you develop a writing career, or simply get some additional reward for your expertise.

Programming ArcGIS 10.1 with Python Cookbook

ISBN: 978-1-84969-444-5   Paperback: 304 pages

Over 75 recipes to help you automate geoprocessing tasks, create solutions, and solve problems for ArcGIS with Python

1. Learn how to create geoprocessing scripts with ArcPy

2. Customize and modify ArcGIS with Python

3. Create time-saving tools and scripts for ArcGIS

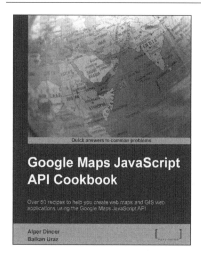

Google Maps JavaScript API Cookbook

ISBN: 978-1-84969-882-5   Paperback: 316 pages

Over 50 recipes to help you create web maps and GIS web applications using the Google Maps JavaScript API

1. Add to your website's functionality by utilizing Google Maps' power

2. Full of code examples and screenshots for practical and efficient learning

3. Empowers you to build your own mapping application from the ground up

Please check **www.PacktPub.com** for information on our titles

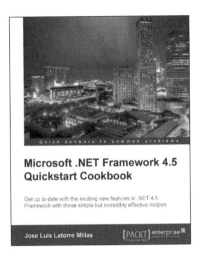
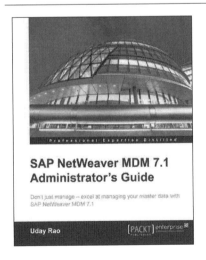